Acclaim for
I DIDN'T FALL, I **|**

MW00395820

This book is a story only a wo~~unded healer can tell. It is a story~~ of redemption and a healing journey that navigates religious identity and spiritual redemption. Dr. Delaney gives readers insight into the layers of healing that survivors of clergy abuse face along the path to transformation and advocacy for others.

> Jaime J. Romo, Ed.D., author, *Healing the Sexually Abused Heart: A Workbook for Survivors, Thrivers, and Supporters* www.jaimeromo.com

Susan's mindfulness brings epiphanies; she generously shares them with us in her book. Spiritual directors and pastoral counselors can learn from Susan's gentle insights.

> Nancy K. Dunkerley, Founding Director, Spiritual Ministries Institute. www.spiritualministriesinstitute.org

The memoir is written as a journal of the author's experience of a retreat at a Benedictine monastery in Pecos, New Mexico, where she studied Spiritual Direction. The story unfolds at monastery pace: structured and slow. The author unhurriedly reveals, in a solid, simple way, the story of her childhood sexual abuse by a Catholic priest, and how she lost and regained her faith after the abuse. Told in down-to-earth yet compelling prose, the memoir will appeal especially to those accustomed to retreats and retreat houses set in a beautiful environment and the spiritual healing that can come with the right retreat, leadership, companions, and surroundings. I strongly recommend this story of hope and healing.

> Frank Douglas, Voice in the Desert, www.reform-network. net

Sexual violation is devastating to the body, to the emotions but also to the soul. The path to healing, which many never complete, is especially steep for the healing of the soul. Susan's gentle and insightful story of her own journey serves as an encouragement to anyone who struggles with the pain of spiritual loss.

Thomas P. Doyle O.P., author, *Sex, Priests and Secret Codes*

This book is absolutely fascinating. During a course of instruction in Spiritual Direction in a Benedictine monastery, Susan embraced a technique for engaging in a dialog between her rational, conscious self and her creative self. The dialog led to a remarkable recognition and understanding of her innermost feelings and to the ability to find forgiveness and healing. This is a fascinating account of her journey from victim to survivor and her ability to apply the words of one of her instructors, "If I am fully aware of God's love for me, I will love me too, and naturally I will love my neighbor." Survivors and their advocates need to put into practice Susan's words, "I hand the thief back his shame."

Steve Sheehan, Publisher, *National Survivor Advocate Coalition* http://nationalsurvivorsadvocatescoalition.wordpress. com

Does sexual abuse of a child by a priest have long-term consequences? Does this abuse compromise the development of spirituality and destroy faith? Can faith be regained and spirituality restored?

Doctor Delaney records her struggle and the process of becoming a healer as she herself was healed. The story is eloquently told and ironically set in a monastery—one of the church's traditional havens to confine abusers—and among the down-and-out homeless, mentally ill. Truly a triumph to lead other wounded persons to the path of healing.

A. W. Richard Sipe, therapist, author, *Sex, Priests and Power*, www.richardsipe.com

Susan has chronicled a very important part of her life. Her efforts to reconnect with her spirituality were challenging but successful. Those looking to reconnect with a "higher power" are encouraged to read this book. The real life story of one woman's journey to wholeness is very readable and inspiring.

Father Bob Hoatson, Road to Recovery, www.road-to-recovery.org

This spiritual memoir is about healing. It is a gift. Susan shares openly about the traumatic effects of being raped by a priest as a little girl. She gives a vivid and precise account of her path to recovery. You feel her hand stretched out, inviting you to find your path. I am grateful for this brave and open-hearted book.

Anne Barrett Doyle, Co-Director, BishopAccountability.org, www.bishopaccountability.org

Susan suffered terrible abuse as a child. Instead of burying her pain, she has chosen to take her experiences and use them to reach out to others who have been injured. Only when survivors like Susan find the courage to speak out will children be safer.

Barb Dorris, SNAP Outreach director, Survivors Network of those Abused by Priests, www.snapnetwork.org

I Didn't Fall, I Was Pushed gives the world a rare but precious window into the wounds, agonies and inner voice of the sexually abused child carried into healing by its adult self. For those who would seek to provide spiritual direction to those who bear the scars of childhood sexual abuse child it is an important guide.

Kristine Ward, Chair, National Survivor Advocates Coalition (NSAC) http://nationalsurvivorsadvocatescoalition.wordpress.com

I DIDN'T FALL, I WAS PUSHED:

Triumphant recovery from clergy sex abuse

by

Susan Delphine Delaney, MD, MS

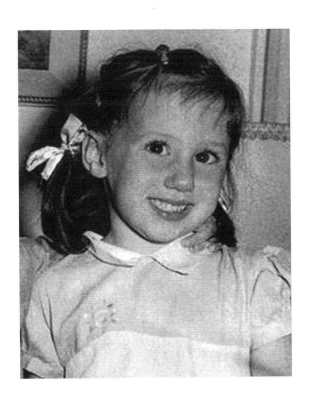

FIRST EDITION

ISBN 978-1-46-806152-9 (Paperback)

DEDICATION

This book is dedicated to all of my sisters and brothers
across the world
who have been physically, emotionally, spiritually and sexually
abused
by religious authority figures.

You know who you are.

May you find your voice and reverse the shame.
May you place the shame
back into the hands of the person to whom it truly belongs.

I hand
the thief
back his shame

Contents

Foreword

This book is a spiritual memoir. It is the story of how I lost my faith after being sexually abused by a Catholic priest. It is also an accounting of the decades-long rebuilding of my faith.

My rebuilt faith is a faith in a God of mercy, compassion and love; my new God bears little resemblance to the vengeful-punishment God of my youth.

I have written this book to offer my encouragement, strength and hope to other survivors who dream of regaining their faith.

Clergy sex abuse, with its combined physical, emotional, spiritual and sexual abuses, causes a shattering of the person's sense of self.

Regaining faith after being shattered is not easy.

The story is set during the six weeks I spent at a Benedictine monastery in Pecos, New Mexico, studying Spiritual Direction. I have a towering stack of handwritten notes, handouts, letters and newsletters from my time at the monastery. These have helped me to stay true to the facts.

I deliberately chose quiet words and repetition in telling the story of my time at the monastery. The stillness and repeated events created a wonderful substrate for my healing. I hope you will enter with me into that stillness and repetition.

Flashbacks during the monastery narrative give glimpses into my back-story.

I have an extraordinary duty of confidentiality to my patients and to my prayer partners. I have taken great pains to tell their stories in a way that blurs the details; I have tried to be true to the message in their stories while rendering the persons unrecognizable.

My abuser was named Father Michael. Whether because of God's sense of humor or His wish to provide me opportunity for growth, there were two Michaels at the monastery.

The monastery had a Father Michael the guest master and builder of a grandfather clock that figures heavily in the story.

For the sake of clarity I mention Pecos' Father Michael only twice, always labeling him in his role as guest master.

All other mentions of "Father Michael" refer to my abuser.

The other Michael in this story was a classmate in the School for Charismatic Spiritual Directors. He became a very good friend; he and I were part of a foursome who spent a lot of time together during the School. Michael had been a Benedictine monk at another monastery for 17 years. He had left that monastery some years before and had been released from his vows by the Vatican.

Pecos was an extraordinarily ecumenical and egalitarian community when I was there in the mid-nineties. No priest, nun or brother expected us to call them by their title; we called them by their first names. Many chose to call the Abbot and the former Abbot by their first names.

For the sake of clarity in identifying monastic Community members, I have chosen to add the person's religious title the first time I mention the person in a chapter. Subsequent mentions in the same chapter will use the person's first name only.

I have placed one of my short Japanese-style poems, a haiku, on the dedication page, one in this section and one at the end of each chapter. Because of the length of the syllables in the English language, we do not use the traditional Japanese 5-7-5 format. Modern English language haiku are about 12 syllables, yielding poems that may be spoken in one breath.

walking down
to the Pecos
to look for haiku

ONE

1995. Pecos Benedictine Monastery. Week I. Sunday

As I waited outside the shower stall for the water to warm, my heart was filled with excitement and joy. After church I would be travelling from my home in Texas to a Benedictine monastery in New Mexico to study Spiritual Direction.

Spiritual Direction is an ancient art, a ministry of compassionate listening to another as the person walks on her journey with the Divine. I was ready to deepen my knowledge of this work.

I turned my face up to receive the fine mist that spilled over the glass walls of the shower. Soon enough, a metallic smell signaled that the water was hot.

As I basked in the delicious warmth of water hitting my shoulders, thousands of sun struck droplets danced around me and enhanced my feeling of joy at the adventure that lay before me.

That feeling came to a screeching halt when I lathered up. I noticed two angry red handprints on my body. One on my left arm. One on my left ribcage. The handprints pointed forward, as if I had been grabbed from behind. The handprints appeared spontaneously; "they came out of nowhere."

I didn't expect this.

In my mind, I was feeling serene about the four weeks I was about to spend at the monastery. Clearly, some part of me was not serene. A part that was insisting I honor my back-story.

For a year, when I was five years old, I was sodomized, nearly every weekend, by my father's Spiritual Director, Father Michael.

Father Michael was a middle-aged priest who taught at a boys' prep school in the Washington, DC area.

Dad and Father Michael were both avid fishermen and fished together every weekend during Washington's nine-month fishing season.

In the spring when I was five, they began to take me with them when they fished. This was when the abuse began. The sodomy split my rectum open, creating permanent damage. Father Michael told me if I told anyone, he would say I was crazy. So I was silent.

Some have asked me "where my parents were." Father Michael "groomed" my parents first. He became special to our family, our "pet" priest. It was a great "honor" to have him in the family. Once he'd groomed my parents to accept him as a desirable addition to our family, he began to groom me, to prepare me for the abuse. He flattered me. He spent time with me. He told me that I was beautiful and smart. The abuse lasted throughout the fishing season when I was five.

In the fishing season when I was seven, Father Michael became my Spiritual Director. We spent endless Saturdays sitting on the banks of the Potomac River; the Anacostia River; the Chesapeake and Ohio Canal and farm ponds. We discussed the fine points of sacramental theology.

Once, he revealed he heard the confessions of the nuns at a convent near to the school where he taught.

"What is that like?" I asked.

"It is like being stoned to death by popcorn," he replied, with a laugh. *Next May, when I am old enough to make my confession, I will stone my confessor to death with popcorn, too.*

Somehow, as I took the first steps on my faith journey, I was able to hold together the paradox of Father Michael's priestly office and the terrible physical, emotional, spiritual and sexual abuse he had committed against me.

One of the ways I dealt with the paradox was to forget the abuse, stuffing it deep into my unconscious mind. Most children who experience traumatic abuse do this same forgetting. It is often the best course of action available to us. Forgetting allowed me to grow in my faith tradition and also to grow spiritually.

4

When I was nine, I started going to 6:30 Mass every morning. Looking back, I see a child determined to grow spiritually and determined to stay safe.

I would walk a block and a half to the church and wait outside for the parish priest to unlock the door. I followed him down the aisle, keeping plenty of distance between us. He headed to the sacristy and I headed for the left front pew. The teaching nuns from my school already filled the first three pews on the right. Each wore a huge set of starched white wings on her head. I took my place in the front pew, in full view of seventeen nuns, my winged protectors. After Mass, I would hightail it out of there and return home for breakfast.

The embrace of paradox served me well until I was 19. I had continued to attend daily Mass at my college, the University of Maryland, College Park. By then, I had completely forgotten the abuse. I would not recall it until I was 41, the year after I came back to faith in Jesus. Like many survivors of clergy sex abuse, I remembered my abuse when my sweet, innocent daughter was the same age I was when I was abused.

One day, during the early spring of my freshman year of college, I'd had a long telephone conversation with my friend Rosemary from the old parish. She had been in contact with a priest from our grade school days. He had, she learned, married the woman he'd been in love with the whole time he served at our parish.

He had not been what he pretended to be.

In that moment, I lost my felt experience of faith. The silent and intensely powerful unconscious memory of abuse by Father Michael reached up and seized hold of my faith, pulling it under the murky waters of my unconscious mind.

My faith had been a joyful and robust faith. Now I plunged into a howling emptiness, devoid of pleasure and imagination. Daily Mass became a time of misery and longing for my former experience of faith. It became too painful to attend daily worship, so I cut my attendance at Mass to times of obligation, such as Sundays and certain feast days.

Perhaps a Spiritual Director could have helped me understand what was happening to me. But of course, a Spiritual Director was the last person I would have turned to.

Over the next four years my attendance at worship declined and then stopped.

I did not fully regain the felt experience of my faith until age 40. I regained my faith in the Creator in medical school, at age 27, seeing His wondrous design in the human body.

I regained my faith in the Holy Spirit during my psychiatric residency, at age 30, as the Spirit began to guide me in figuring out what to say to my therapy patients.

I did not begin to regain my faith in Jesus until I was 37 when I began to attend an Episcopal church. I started attending church again so that my daughter could go to Sunday school and get a moral education. Slowly the recitation of the prayers, and especially of the creed, began to awaken my faith in Jesus. By age 40 my faith in Jesus was pretty secure.

Now, at 47, as I planned my trip to the monastery, I judged that my faith was strong and unassailable. I felt I was ready to leave the abuse behind me and "boldly go" into a monastery heavily populated with Spiritual Director priests.

The red handprints informed me there was a part of me that was not OK with being at a monastery. A part of me that still needed healing. That part of me produced the handprints. The handprints, with fingers pointing forward, mirrored the way that Father Michael had grabbed me when he sodomized me.

The angry red handprint on my ribcage would fade within the week. The sunburn I got that morning at the outdoor worship service at my home church turned the handprint on my upper arm into four battle stripes I would wear until winter.

The morning of my departure, at church, I saw 35 friends who had promised to pray for me daily during the School. All already had my photo on their fridges.

Only one asked me about the fire-y handprint on my arm.

Physically surrounded by my church family, I felt utterly alone. Those of us who have been abused physically, emotionally, spiritually or sexually live inside a wall of silence. The wall is created by our family, friends, teachers and religious leaders. The wall confines us within the story written about us by others. Others who do not care to know the truth of our lives. Others who do not care to know the truth of our abusers' lives.

After the church service, I went home to change from my sleeveless dress into something more "modest." At the monastery, none of us would be allowed to wear shorts or sleeveless tops.

I would spend the next four weeks at the monastery during the summer of 1995 and two weeks during the summer of 1996.

The monastery is a double monastery; one consisting of priest and brother monks; the other, monastic nuns.

My classmates and I, 33 of us in all, would live at the monastery, worshiping three times a day with the monastic community and taking our meals with them. We would have 60 hours of instruction that summer and 30 the next.

At the time, my daughter was just 12. I had not planned on going to the monastery until Sarah was in college. However, at breakfast one day in the previous spring, I told Sarah and her dad, my husband of 16 years, of my longing to study Spiritual Direction at Pecos.

Sarah told her best friend Robin; Robin told her mom Linda. Linda called me and said, "Go, I will take care of your daughter." I felt immediate peace. I filled out my application and sent it in. I was accepted by return mail.

As I prepared for the trip, things fell into place. Sarah and Robin were invited to assist a summer school teacher at the school close to our home. Linda would keep Sarah every night. She'd drop the girls at my house on her way to work. The girls would walk five doors to the school an hour later. After helping the teacher, they would walk back to my house and stay there until Linda picked up Robin after work. Sarah would stay and have dinner with her dad, then go over to Robin's for the night.

I had written Sarah a letter for every day I would be gone and had enclosed one or more photos. The box of letters, each written on a different type of stationery, was already at Robin's. Sarah, in turn, had made me an audiotape, with a recording for each day, with at least one photo.

I felt good about the plan. Sarah would spend time every morning and night with a woman she regarded as a second mom. And she would have time with her dad every day. She and I would talk by phone every day.

A glitch would leave me anxious during my last days at home and during my first few days at the monastery. On the Thursday before my departure, Sarah and Robin were practicing forward flips into the pool. Sarah smacked her nose against the side of the pool. X-rays showed she had broken off a thin crescent of bone on the right side of her nose.

The otolaryngologist, who had treated Sarah many times before, was reassuring. He showed me how he was going to push the bone back into place. It would only take him 45 seconds. The main risk, he said, was the anesthesia.

No kidding, I thought to myself. I had a cardiac arrest during my tonsillectomy in the winter of my fifth year. I had gone to heaven for a while. *What if Sarah dies during surgery, like I did? Would she come back?*

My best friend, JoAnn, grandmother of five, agreed to be with Sarah before and after her surgery and to keep her the rest of the day, feeding her lunch and dinner and taking her to the healing service at our church that night.

The surgery was scheduled for Tuesday, my third day at the monastery.

It's only 45 seconds, I kept telling myself. *JoAnn will be with her all day. Sarah will be OK. I will be OK.*

All plans were in place. My anxiety was at bay. I was modestly dressed. My family set off for the airport. In those days your family could come right up to the gate with you.

"Don't go," Sarah said at the gate. *Fifty times.*

But I was at peace. I knew that I was to go and I knew Sarah would be fine; beyond that, she would be taken care of by people who loved her. She and I would talk by phone every day.

My flight was called. I boarded the aircraft and found my seat for the hour and fifty minute flight to Albuquerque. During the preflight instructions, I clutched my spiral notebook, whose cover was bright red with an all-over holographic design. The notebook was blank except for the photos of the 51 people who would be praying for me every day. Thirty-five were from my church, 16 were family members. Their photos were pasted inside of the back cover of the notebook.

After takeoff, cocooned by the white noise of the jet engines, I rocked my red notebook back and forth in the sunbeam for a moment, enjoying the changing holographic design. It threw tiny red sunbeams all across my chest, the wall of the plane and the seatback in front of me. I began to write in the notebook, beginning the journal that would become this book.

The clouds were beautiful that day; big, fluffy, fair-weather clouds. My joy was back. I didn't like the handprints, I didn't like leaving my daughter behind to face surgery without me, but I was keenly aware I was where I was supposed to be and Sarah and I would both be OK.

Mid-flight, I looked up and yawned. A fine spray of water droplets shot out from under my tongue, lit up by the sunbeam that was already warming me. *It's going to be OK.*

Soon I heard the gears cranking the wing flaps for landing and with a small bump we touched down, right on time.

My baggage was not on time, however. It took 30 minutes to arrive at the carousel. By then I had missed my bus to Santa Fe, where a monastic community member was waiting to pick me up.

I waited 90 minutes for the next Shuttlejack. The driver sold me my ticket, a roughly-scissored two-inch square.

I climbed aboard and spied a smiling white-haired pixie in the seat behind the driver's. She looked so friendly that I sat down beside her and introduced myself. She was Bette Ann, an Episcopalian like me, and she was headed for the monastery. Like me, she was involved in the healing ministry. We were BFF (Best Friends Forever) instantly. The seventy-five minute ride to Santa Fe passed in a flash as we got to know each other. Before we knew it the driver was dropping us at the Inn at Loreto in downtown Santa Fe.

The tiny blue station wagon that the monastery had sent for the next arrival group was full. I had to sit between the bucket seats on top of the gear shift and the parking brake. The earthy nun who drove us would warn me every time she shifted, "Now I am not getting fresh, I am shifting." The pain in my tailbone was made bearable by my excitement at getting closer to the monastery.

After a 25-minute drive, we turned between two adobe pillars into the monastery grounds. Under a cluster of three tall fir trees was a statue of Mary, the Mother of God, depicted as Our Lady of Guadalupe. A crown of fresh roses was woven around her concrete crown. Many rosaries were draped around her praying hands. We pulled up in front of the two-story adobe monastery with its four-story bell tower. Disembarking, I stretched and creaked into an upright position.

Inside, a beaming Australian priest, Father Michael, greeted me. *Of course it would have to be a Father Michael. Breathe, Susan, just breathe.* It was impossible to remain upset in the face of his cheery greeting. He handed me my room key and a sheaf of papers with the housekeeping information I would need for my four-week stay. He also gave me the syllabus for the summer's study.

My room, number 19, was on the road side of the guesthouse. It had a two-part sliding picture window opening onto the hallway. The beige curtains were open. The cinder-brick walls were painted a soft butter yellow. A single bed was against the left wall, my desk and dresser against the right wall. My bathroom, with sink, tub and shower, was in the back of the room. The bathroom was painted warm beige; the tiles were speckled oatmeal in color.

I set about unpacking my suitcase. That summer I would be a khakis and tee shirt gal. I'd brought socks to match each tee, as well as matching two-yard lengths of grosgrain ribbon to tie through the loops of the khakis as belts.

I unpacked a stack of ironed handkerchiefs. The average woman cries three times a week. I am an above average woman. I always carry two clean handkerchiefs, one in each pocket of my khakis. One for me and one for any friend who may be crying.

I placed my multicolored Koosh ball on the dresser; I thought it would be fun to toss around with my classmates during breaks. My motto was, "Anyone can catch it; anyone can drop it."

I set my three juggle balls beside it; I'd had them for years and wanted to master juggling while I was at the monastery.

As I fluffed the stuffed "prayer pig," Petunia, that Sarah had given me, the plastic pellets that weighted her feet made a crunching sound. I unpacked 20 photos of my family. I used teacher's sticky-putty to affix them to the wall behind my desk. This instantly broke the rule about putting anything on the walls.

Have I left Catholic guilt behind me?

I lifted a deep green box from my suitcase, tenderly running my fingers over the fabric-like embossing. Inside were 90 quilt squares, each ready to have a coordinating heart appliquéd onto it. I was working on a quilt for Sarah. Each square would become a prayer for her.

Within a few moments of having finished unpacking, the bell in the tower called us to dinner with the monks and monastic nuns. It would be our first turkey meal, turkey meatloaf with carrots and broccoli, and a baked potato.

Turkey would be the only meat served at the monastery during the four weeks. We would have turkey spaghetti sauce, turkey meatballs, turkey Salisbury steak, turkey burgers, and other turkey dishes mercifully relegated to my unconscious mind, where they reside with other traumas.

After dinner, we moved downstairs to our classroom for a brief overview of our course of study.

Immediately following this, the -monks and nuns joined us for a reception. I met the rest of my classmates. Twenty three of us were women; ten were men. About 50% were Catholic, including two priests, a brother from the Pecos community and two nuns from other religious orders. A good number of us were

Episcopalians, including laypersons like myself, a seminarian, and the wife of an Episcopal priest. We also had lay Lutherans, two Baptist ministers and a Disciples of Christ minister.

The members of the monastic community greeted each of us by name. Amazingly, each monastic knew who each of us was and what we did "out there in the world."

Also present at the reception were the Oblates serving during the school. An Oblate is a person, lay, clerical, single or married, who is formally associated with a particular monastery. Benedictine Oblates seek to live within the contemporary expression of the Rule of St. Benedict, both when in residence at the monastery and when at home. Oblates generally are in residence at the monastery 1-3 weeks a year. When in residence they perform "tasks as assigned."

I met Carole, an Oblate serving during the school. She was a friend of my friend Sheila Linn. I knew from Sheila that Carole and I would click because Carol was a quilter, in the healing ministry, and had had a Near Death Experience (NDE). Carole and I made plans to get together a few days later.

My Spiritual Director for the School, Sister Debbie, introduced herself, as did Brother Ed, the monastery photographer and audio taper. Ed was looking for me. He grew up in the community just south of my home in Texas.

During a chat with Bette Ann, I met Michael, a fortyish former Benedictine monk who had been released from his Benedictine vows by the Vatican. He was currently in the lay state but planned to join another religious order at the end of the School.

After the reception, we all repaired to the chapel to read Compline, a bedtime monastic office (service). I sat with Bette Ann, my new BFF, and Michael, the former monk. *Of course it would be another Michael.* By then, I was resigned to dealing with the "Michael thing." *He seems to be kind and a gentleman.*

Back in my room, I closed my windows and my curtains for the night and listened to the tape that Sarah had made for the day. On the tape, she'd worried that the airplane food would be awful. She couldn't have known when she made the tape that I'd carry onboard a delightful meal of a half-pint of milk and the blueberry buckle that she and I had made the night before. I af-fixed to the wall the two photos she'd included with her tape.

Exhausted by all of the different venues I had faced that day, I grabbed my prayer pig and fell asleep as soon as my head touched the pillow.

don't go
don't go
don't go

TWO

1995, Pecos Benedictine Monastery, Week I, Monday

I opened my eyes a few minutes before my 5 a.m. alarm sounded.

I am here. I am here. I am finally here!

For seven years I'd listened to friends, lay and clergy, talk about their time at Pecos' School for Charismatic Spiritual Directors, and how they had come away healed and changed. Within hours of telling my family of my desire to study here, my wish-coming-true had begun to unfold.

Now, I lay in the dark, taking grateful breaths of clean mountain air. Birdsong had not begun, but bugsong was in full chorus. My heart soared with each crescendo.

When my alarm began to chirp, I switched it off and turned on my desk light. Sitting at the desk, I looked at each of the 22 photos I had affixed to the wall; I drew each one anew into my heart.

I began to review the syllabus with its list of classes; the daily schedule; the laundry and library rules. There was also a short biography of each monastic. As you might expect for a monastery in New Mexico, most of the monks and nuns were from Midwestern or Western states. A few were from farther afield: London, Australia and Italy.

Birdsong heralded the coming of daylight at six. The light told me that Pecos was positioned at a place in its time zone that would allow me to take a long walk before the morning worship service. I resolved to explore the walking trails and to find a walking buddy.

I paused to say a special prayer for my brother, Peter, who has Down syndrome. Today was his forty-second birthday.

I took a luxuriously long warm shower and dressed, waiting until the normal people were up at 6.30 a.m., to blow-dry my hair.

I was looking forward to the day's complete tour of the monastery and grounds. I had had a brief tour of the monastery a year before. The monastery had sponsored a three-day retreat given by my friends Father Matthew Linn and Dennis and Sheila Linn. The retreat had been held at a nearby Baptist encampment. The abbreviated tour had included the chapel, classroom and the monastery's Dove Publications, a divinely huge bookstore.

During the 1994 Linn retreat, I had a brief conversation with Pecos' Sister Theresa. I vividly remember my soft, introvert voice making her draw back. This was my first clue that the monastery was a wholly different planet from our own.

After a quick peek at the clock, I lay down, closed my eyes and let birdsong wash over me. Just before seven, I padded down the hallway to the chapel. Morning light shone through huge windows. Random panes of solid red and solid blue glass added mystery and a hush of reverence to the sacred space. Rows of chairs with metal frames stretched along each wall near the entrance door; the chairs had padded backs and seats. These were for the School participants and visitors. Nearer to the altar were two groupings of chairs. One, to the left, was for Catholic priests celebrating the Mass along with the main celebrant; the chairs on the right were for the rest of the monastic community, brothers and nuns.

Behind the altar was a twelve-foot mural of ceramic tile, created by a visiting female monastic. It portrayed the Risen Christ. He had four concentric halos. Golden rods extended beyond the mural, representing beams of light streaming from the halos. The Christ figure was portrayed graphically, as is common in Catholic art. Streams of red and golden blood flowed from the wounds in his hands and side. Most of the composition was in reds, golds, turquoises and blacks. The monastic artist had also incorporated a few shards of a broken brown coffee mug from the dining room. On my previous brief visit, I had learned that many physical and emotional healings had occurred when people touched this mural.

16

On the left wall was a painted mural of Our Lady of Guadalupe, the patron saint of the monastery. I chose a seat on the wall, near this mural. I noted that there was a box of Kleenex under each seat.

My kind of place! They "get" crying. In the Eastern Orthodox Christian churches, the "Gift of Tears," is regarded as one of the gifts of the Holy Spirit. Most of my tears were tears of wonder and gratitude.

Bette Ann and Michael soon joined me. Michael gave us the first hint of his crackpot sense of humor. "Are they praying again?"

Soon the monastic community arrived, dressed in their white Olivetan Benedictine robes, and took their places near the altar. One, Sister Geralyn, began to play her guitar. Soon she was leading us in Praise songs. My mood returned to the joy I had felt earlier at bugsong. My heart swelled and my face lifted upward in joy.

Abbot David celebrated the Mass. Abbot David had been one of the founders of the monastery in 1969, and had founded the School in 1978. He had moved on to become the Abbot at the Monastery of the Risen Christ in San Luis Obispo, California in 1992, but had returned for four weeks to help teach.

At the Passing of the Peace, I learned that it was the custom to pass the Peace of Christ to every single person in the room. That meant "peacing" 64 other people: 32 other students, 23 monastics, 3 resident Oblates, 1 volunteer Oblate and 5 Oblates serving as School assistants. Passing the Peace took at least 15 minutes.

We negotiated the Passing of the Peace with incredible respect and gentleness. One would want a bear hug, another wanted a stiff-armed hug, yet another wanted a handshake. This respect would be very important as the School went on and issues were stirred up in each of us. The "Peace" that was good for a person yesterday might be overwhelming today.

The Abbot invited us to voice aloud any special intentions for prayer. I desperately wanted to ask the community to pray for Sarah's surgery the next day, but I was unable to open my mouth. I resolved to write a note to Abbot Andrew and ask him to do it for me the next morning.

The monastery took seriously the charge of Vatican II that to be a good Catholic, you had to be ecumenical. The monks did a quiet end run around the "only Catholics can take communion" in two ways. They asked us to receive only if we believed in the true presence of Jesus in communion. And they got the nuns to give out communion, a gracious and charitable compassion for those of us who were Episcopalians, Disciples of Christ, Baptists, and Lutherans.

After Mass, we all repaired to the dining room on the second floor, just above our classroom. In accordance with the Rule of St. Benedict, a wide variety of foods was available. Many types of cereal, two kinds of bran, milk, yogurt and several types of fruit made for a wonderful smorgasbord. Father Paul, who bore an uncanny resemblance to my abuser, whispered to me that the oat bran was a lot easier on the digestion than the wheat bran.

I sat with Brother Ed, who had introduced himself the night before at the reception. He asked me why I had come to the School. "I want to get healed," I replied, "I see the School as a residential treatment center for the folks at the top of the food chain." Ed burst out laughing, spraying the table with coffee. "Not many people get that," he said, when he could breathe again.

After breakfast, we clomped down the steps to the classroom. It was a huge room with a massive stone fireplace. Five rows of caramel leather, movie-theater-style seats filled the center of the room, eight seats to a row. A center aisle divided each row. Each chair was stitched with an intricate cowboy motif, a legacy from the monastery's dude ranch past.

Earlier, I had selected an upholstered straight back chair against the back wall, in the sun, and my green box of 90 quilt squares and 90 fat hearts was already waiting for me. Nestled among the squares and hearts was a baggie with scissors, pins, needles and thread.

Pecos was a psychologically minded monastery. Its philosophy was heavily influenced by the work of Swiss psychiatrist Carl Jung. I knew that a lot of what would be taught would be very familiar to me so I'd brought quilt squares to stitch on during those classes.

I settled down and watched each of my classmates find a place among the cowboy seats. No one else chose the back row.

Abbot David began by telling us that the monastery was a safe place for us, a place where we could share our deepest selves. He pointed out there was a box of Kleenex under every chair.

"Let us see what God will do here."

The School was grounded in Scripture and in the working of the Holy Spirit. It was his hope, and that of the monastic community, that we would grow in the Holy Spirit while we were there, and as a result surrender in a deeper way to the working of God in our lives.

"You were called here to study Spiritual Direction; Spiritual Direction is a gift, a charism. Pray for a deepening of that gift within you," he said.

The monastic community, he explained, was a loving one, sanctified by their attempt to treat one another and the students as if each were Christ. This earnest intention was designed to bring each of us, monk and student alike, into a deeper, more primary relationship with God.

"A sunflower recognizes the source of its energy and follows it," he said, "We want to help you do the same thing." This metaphor meant a lot to me. Sarah's little face had followed me like a sunflower when she was small. Each of the first five cards in the box of letters I had left for her had sunflowers on the front; each card was different.

The monastery believed in a holistic approach to spirituality: regular worship, wholesome food, and exercise. We would also nourish our spirits with prayer, journaling, and creative expression.

We had a short break before the tour. I raced to my room to write a note to Carole asking for her prayers for Sarah and me. I slipped a piece of waxy blue carbon paper into my notebook underneath the notepaper so that I could keep a copy of my plea.

Dear Carole,

I am writing to ask your prayers today and in the morning.

My twelve year old, Sarah, has broken her nose and will have very simple surgery tomorrow morning at 7 a.m. CST to correct the fracture.

She is missing her mommy, who has always been there for her.

I feel her pain. Sheila has told me you had a Near Death Experience. I died during my tonsillectomy at age 5. I fear a similar death for Sarah.

I know I am supposed to be here. I trust God. But Sarah and I are hurting.

Please pray God's peace and protection for us.

Thank You,

Susan Delphine Delaney – Room #19

I folded the note and stuck a two-inch piece of Scotch tape to my finger. I walked toward the chapel and zigged right at the end of the hallway. When I got to Carole's room I taped the note to her door then zagged left at the long main hallway leading past the bell tower, past the chapel and on into the classroom. We would begin our tour there.

Sister Clare, the nun who had given me a brief tour on my previous visit to the monastery, was our tour guide. Today we learned that the monastery property, about 900 acres, was nestled in the Sangre de Cristo Mountains. The Pecos River ran through it. After its run as a dude ranch, the property had belonged to a Benedictine congregation who had hoped to farm the land. When they discovered the high altitude made farming impractical, the first community of monks transferred the monastery, Our Lady of Guadalupe Abbey, to "our" monks. The current congregation of monks had been, from the first, a deliberate part of the Catholic Charismatic Renewal.

We started the tour with a visit to a very important room, the break room, just off the classroom. Light from six windows flooded the tables and chairs. Coffee and tea were available, as well as little packets of graham crackers. The graham crackers would become essential to me, both for snacking and for feeding the resident ducklings. A pay phone was in a little booth. Against the wall were our mailboxes and the outgoing mail tray.

The bulletin board contained an ominous cartoon: a man is being turned back by Saint Peter, who says, "I'm sorry, you simply chose the wrong religion." My stomach twisted into a knot when I saw it.

Outside, we crossed the driveway and moved up a slight grade toward the adobe pillars of the entrance to the monastery grounds. I saw that the pillars each had three stair-like steps. A small adobe building was just inside the gates; the gift shop consisted of four small rooms that once made up a Pony Express station. The shop was filled with sparkling glass ornaments, books, leaflets and many items handmade by members of the monastic community. Outside the gift shop was a cottonwood tree. I could hear the distinctive rustle of its leaves as I passed.

We moved downhill to cross a small laughing brook, which dove into a culvert beneath our feet. Daisy, the monastery dog, toddled over to meet us. A short, stocky brown dog of mixed heritage, she greeted us with a quiet enthusiasm. Clare told us desserts were only served on feast days and on Community members' birthdays. The monks had petitioned Abbot Andrew to have Daisy's birthday added to their birthday roster, meaning one extra dessert each year. Unfortunately, he had turned down their request.

Ascending a small slope, we entered Dove Publications, the monastery bookstore and press. The monks sold hundreds of titles. The books were stacked on warehouse shelves. I longed to stay behind with the books, but gamely followed Clare to the monastery side of the Dove building, into the gymnasium. Here, we would have our twice-weekly workouts with a monk who was a certified fitness trainer.

Leaving the gym and continuing downhill, we saw the cottages occupied by the resident oblates, then three in number: a married couple and a single woman. We followed a dirt road on a slight downhill incline toward the river. The laughing brook bubbled beside the road. The brook was lined with trees nourished by its waters. At the end of the road was a duck pond, replete with a speckled brown mallard and her four tiny ducklings. Straight ahead I could see a footbridge over the Pecos, leading to another mountain.

The laughing brook dove into another culvert and then entered the Pecos. Turning right over the buried culvert, we followed the rutted dirt road along the river, which sang with high water. When we came to the woods Clare showed us the narrow trail to the waterfall upriver. Turning right again, we followed the road in a sweeping turn back to the monastery, passing the orchards and the bee hives. We passed the nuns' dormitory and came back to the guesthouse. Clare left us to rest before lunch.

When I got back to my room, I found Carole's reply to my note.

Dear Susan,

I received your note when I came back to my room during our kitchen break.

I certainly will pray for you and your daughter, Sarah.

You still are there for her and in a very powerful way through prayer.

I, too, can feel your pain and Sarah's pain. Surgery must be an extra anxious time for you in light of your experience. I hope we can share. Maybe after one of these meals.

Believe it. I'm praying.

Carole

I breathed a prayer of gratitude and relief. *She gets me!* I taped her note into my notebook.

Lunch was the ever-present turkey, this time served as turkey salad sandwiches and a green salad.

The afternoon was given over to our first meetings with our Spiritual Directors. Mine was scheduled for 2.30 p.m. in the library on the lower level under the chapel. I descended the stairs to a large open lounge with picture windows that framed the Pecos Valley. The room had several groupings of couches and chairs. The library was a glassed-in room in the back corner of the lounge.

Sister Debbie was on time. She offered me her hand in welcome. Her biography had described her studies in Psychology and Nutrition, two of my great interests.

We sat in silence for a moment and then I began by stating my goals for healing during the School. I explained that I wanted to forgive two people; to forgive God for sending me back to Earth during my Near Death Experience (NDE); to experience the joy that usually comes from the Baptism of the Holy Spirit and to reconnect with my fondness for Mary, the Mother of God.

I shared my concern for Sarah's surgery in the morning. I mentioned my Near Death Experience as a child and my fears that Sarah would die in surgery, too. She asked me to recount the NDE I had at the end of my fifth year.

I was lying on a cold operating table, clothed only in my underpants and covered by a thin sheet. The senior doctor had placed a domed, screened mask over my mouth and nose and covered it with a piece of gauze. He held a glass bottle of clear fluid in his hand. "Breathe in, this will smell sweet," he said. He began to pour ether onto the gauze. I breathed in the sickly sweet smell. Suddenly I was up on the ceiling, watching the senior doctor and his younger assistant. The senior doctor was still dribbling ether onto the mask.

"She is so little, aren't you afraid of overdosing her?" the resident doctor asked. "I don't care if I kill her!" the senior doctor replied.

"Too late!" I thought from my perch on the ceiling. I was in a place of peace, warmth and safety. And that horrible smell was gone. I felt mercy and compassion for the doctor, even though I knew his words were wrong-headed. Then there was a tunnel and at the end of it a wonderful place with glowing flowers. The flowers shone with their own emitted light.

Then I woke up. Mother was with me, holding a curved metal pan to my mouth; I was vomiting blood. I remember thinking that it looked a lot like Campbell's tomato soup.

Ether is renowned for causing the heart to stop. Likely this happened, sending me to heaven briefly.

I have never been able to get worked up over the doctor's remarks. I have always accepted them and I have always sent love his way.

That experience of infused compassion in the face of such ugliness shaped my attitude toward the world. Somehow the safety and comfort that enfolded me on the ceiling gave me a lifelong inclination to compassion and forgiveness.

Debbie reminded me that I would have to write two book reports for graduation the next summer. She recommended that I consider reading two books about Near Death Experiences from the official School reading list. I could write the book reports required for graduation the next summer about these books. She recommended *Love is the Link* by Pamela Kircher MD, a hospice physician who had a childhood NDE; and *Beyond the Mirror* by Father Henri Nouwen, who had his NDE as an adult. Both, she said, were available at the small bookstore, just off the classroom.

We agreed to meet twice a week at 2:30 p.m., usually on Tuesdays and Thursdays.

I hot-footed it back to my room and composed my note to Abbot Andrew:

Abbot Andrew,

I was too uncomfortable to speak up this morning at Eucharist (Mass).

My daughter, Sarah, 12, has broken her nose and will have a brief surgical procedure to repair it tomorrow morning during our Eucharist.

Would you speak for me and lift her up before the community?

Thank You,

Susan Delphine Delaney

On the way to the break room, I saw a monk and asked him to put my note in Abbot Andrew's box.

After thanking him, I proceeded to the break room and brewed a cup of tea. I carried the tea and two packages of graham crackers to a table in a sunbeam, and gazed toward the laughing brook. The cottonwoods were shedding inch-wide fluffy particles, "cottonwood duff," that looked for all the world like snow. Each particle of duff was backlit by the sun and glowed with light. I watched in wonder and gratitude as I sat in the warm sunbeam and sipped my tea. I slipped the graham crackers into my pocket.

I looked at my watch. Bette Ann would be back in her room after her Spiritual Direction. I knocked on her door. Her room was along the long central hallway of the monastery. Her windows faced the Pecos River Valley. She gave me an enthusiastic hug when she opened the door. I invited her to walk along the river with me. She was delighted to accompany me. She was dressed, as always, in a pristine white knit skirt that matched her crown of white hair. Her Mickey Mouse watch had a red band that matched her red belt.

We stopped at the duck pond to feed the ducklings graham crackers. We meandered along the river road and entered the wooded trail to the waterfall. The woods were sparse. Sun sparkled on the river. The trail was lined with straight, segmented horsetail plants. We saw a chest-high pine that had lost its head and had grown back two in its place. I saluted the pine's determination to survive despite a terrible wound. We came to the "waterfall," which was a cascade of splashing, joyful water where the river dropped about three feet.

"Bette Ann," I said, "I would like to invite you to join me on a walk each morning at 6:00 a.m."

"Ah, Susan," she said, "you must call me BA, like my friends do back home, and no, I cannot walk with you. For me there is only one 6 o'clock everyday, 6 p.m."

We walked back slowly, talking with the earnestness of BBFs. We passed the orchard with its beehives. Clare, our tour guide, was propped against an apple tree reading a murder mystery. We waved and moved on. As we approached the guesthouse, the bell sounded for Vespers, a late afternoon monastic service. We joined Michael in the chairs near the Guadalupe mural. Our new friend Coy was at the end of the row, in the corner. He was a Disciples of Christ Minister. We nodded as we passed.

After Vespers, we were off to the dining room for a new taste sensation: turkey Salisbury steak with green beans and poppy-studded buttered noodles.

A dark thought entered my mind. *I wonder if that Nutritionist Spiritual Director of mine is responsible for all of this turkey.*

Already missing the daily three-mile walk that I always took at home, I resolved to walk each morning before Eucharist.

I spoke with Sarah before our evening class. I gave her the emergency number for the monastery and prayed with her on the phone. She promised to call me as soon as she got home after surgery. She was very excited about spending the day with my friend JoAnn.

Class that evening was taught by Sister Geralyn, our monastic musician. She discussed our inner journey towards God. She spoke of five techniques to move us closer to the God within us: stillness, prayer, dream-work, journaling and creative expression. I do not think any of us in the class was yet aware that these five things, plus worship, good nutrition and exercise would be the foundation of our time at the monastery and the vehicle that would carry us to the state where we would become inhabitants of Planet Pecos.

Exhausted, I retired to my room. I listened to the tape that Sarah had made for Monday and sticky-puttied the two new pictures she'd included to the wall above my desk.

Climbing into bed, I prayed for peace and safety for Sarah; good rest for her surgeon and for her anesthesiologist. I curled myself around the stuffed pig and fell into a deep sleep.

overcast day
sunflowers
still follow the sun

THREE

1995, Pecos Benedictine Monastery, Week I, Tuesday

When my alarm chirped at 5:30 a.m., I turned it off and lay there enjoying bugsong for a few minutes, then arose and entered my bathroom. I disrobed and inspected the handprints on my arm and ribs. The one on my ribcage was beginning to fade. The one on my upper arm was browning into four battle stripes. I warmed the shower and stepped in. I stood under the spray, enjoying the speckled oatmeal tiles, which made a nice color harmony with the tan walls. I towel dried my hair, preferring not to awaken my hall mates with the loud whine of a blow dryer.

Just before six, I strode down the hall and slid out the back door, which faced the river. I crossed silently behind the cloister, respectful of monks who were still sleeping. I took the dirt road to the river.

Fingers of mist arose from the duck pond. The four ducklings were already awake, peeping asynchronously. Their mother plunged her head to the pond's bottom and pulled up a strand of algae. I turned along the river, following the dirt road, enjoying the river's song, made louder by last night's rain. At the trailhead I plunged into the woods. The loamy trail was squishy from the rain. As I walked I mulled over my Near Death Experience and my concerns about Sarah's surgery that morning. The waterfall laughed and gurgled with high water. I paused beside the waterfall and prayed for Sarah's safety and for successful surgery. I felt great peace.

As I meandered back, I saw a muddy puddle being fed by swirls of fresh, clear water, a freshet from last night's rain. I watched for a moment. *I hope that my muddy soul will be cleansed by a clear, infilling freshet during the School.* I was back at the guesthouse in plenty of time for worship. I went to my room to clean the mud off of my shoes and to switch to my ancient brown leather Birkenstocks.

I was able to return to the great peace I felt about Sarah when Abbot Andrew lifted her up before the community for me.

At breakfast, I was surprised to feel ongoing peace. I sat with BA, Michael and Coy. Soon I saw Carole hurrying to me, beckoning.

"Your daughter is on the phone!" she said, "She sounds good!"

Carole, in the kitchen preparing food for lunch, had listened for the phone, knowing that Sarah would call.

"Hi, Mom, it went great! I am awake and JoAnn is with me. Dad already left." She chattered on about the games she had played with Joann while waiting for surgery.

"JoAnn is going to take me to the healing service tonight. I am so excited!"

She put JoAnn on the line. "Well, I am sure that you can tell that she is perfectly well. I will be taking her to your house as soon as they release her."

I thanked JoAnn from the bottom of my heart and hung up. Tears of gratitude welled up in my eyes.

I thanked Carole for her kindness. She gave me a big hug.

"I didn't want you to have to listen to a voicemail; I wanted you to be able to speak directly to your daughter."

Carole and I agreed to meet late Thursday afternoon to talk and get to know each other better.

I rejoined my friends, eyes still leaking a little. BA gave me a big hug.

Listening to my friend's conversation, I learned that the Abbot Andrew, the current superior, was staying in the guesthouse, just four doors down from me. Apparently this was partly so he could keep an eye on the 33 of us. He also wanted, the story went, to keep an eye on our lecturers. The lectures were piped into all of our rooms, so that we might hear them even if we were indisposed. The Abbot wanted to monitor the lectures to make sure that our teachers stayed on message.

After breakfast several other clusters of new friends talked earnestly as we all moved downstairs to our classroom.

I took my place in the window row and bent my head over my appliqué. My uncapped pen and my open notebook were in the chair to my right.

Abbot David was our first morning lecturer. His topic was "Catechesis and Christian Renewal."

He exhorted us to trust God, and to trust one another.

"A community can love an unlovable person that one person could not love alone."

He spoke of how the shared task of loving a difficult person lightened the load of any one person. Living in community was still a daily "crucifixion" but the task was made easier by being shared.

I saw my friend Michael, a veteran of 17 years in a nearby Benedictine monastery, nodding vigorously.

Could it be that Pecos is such a holy and healing place simply because the monks are TRYING to be Christ to one another and to us?

Abbot David spoke of families today and how families do not allow for the broken. Society does not allow for the broken. Society gives you three days off if a loved one dies and you are expected to be back at work firing on eight cylinders.

I am so grateful for my family. Most of us have problems, but we always went as slow as the slowest person. We always informed a baby if we were going to move his stroller. We always informed one another if we were about to make a big noise.

The Abbot gave a history of charismatic phenomena in Scripture. He surprised me by saying that the first he had heard of the modern speaking in tongues was among Sufi Muslims and among Buddhists. Later, this gift of the Holy Spirit was reclaimed by Catholic Christians in the Charismatic Revival. Today, many types of Christians exercise the gift of tongues as a private prayer language, and occasionally in public worship services.

The Abbot encouraged us to experience the Living God in music of all kinds and in nature. An early Catholic theologian, Thomas Aquinas, said that nature is "radiant" with God's image.

The Abbot said something that I would hear again and again during my six weeks at the monastery: the Holy Spirit is present whenever two people try to communicate.

Two monastics, Sister Therese and Sister Geralyn taught the next morning class. "Baptism in the Holy Spirit and Charism."

They spoke of the unique bouquet of spiritual gifts that each of us has. Each of these gifts can be called a "charism." Earlier, we had been told that we each had been called to the School because we had the charism of Spiritual Direction and that we should pray for an increase in this gift. The nuns encouraged us to pray for an increase in each one of our spiritual gifts. Some of the gifts they mentioned were especially interesting to me: wisdom, counsel, piety, ministry and healing.

The nuns spoke in a beautiful, choreographed tandem about Baptism in the Holy Spirit. This is, ideally, they said, what should happen to each of us when we are confirmed. It is a powerful, perceptible infilling of the presence of God, and is almost always accompanied by an ecstatic experience of joy.

I sighed. *I can speak in tongues all right, but I sure wish I could feel that joy.* I knew that tomorrow night we would have a service when we would renew our Baptism vows and our Confirmation vows. *Maybe the joy will finally happen for me tomorrow.*

Lunch was turkey burgers on buns with lettuce, tomato and onion. The four of us, BA, Michael, Coy and I sat together again.

"This turkey is getting OLD," said Michael, voicing what each of us was feeling. We began to plan a jailbreak for Thursday, two days away. We would go to Harry's Roadside Diner in Santa Fe for a late breakfast and beg for some cholesterol. Coy would be our getaway driver. We would slip out after breakfast and return before Spiritual Direction that afternoon. We all left the dining room with big grins on our faces. *Only two more days and we can have some cholesterol!*

With an hour to go before any of us had an appointment, we decided to walk together. We approached the huge, thick, wooden double doors that opened into the classroom. Each door was carved with a lovely, curvy descending dove. We pushed open one of the heavy doors and stepped onto a huge rectangular flat stone the width of both doors that served as a doorstep. Then we moved onto the sunlit dirt driveway.

Daisy, the monastery dog, came up to greet us. Her foot was bleeding! I squatted down. She let me hold it and I prayed aloud for healing. BA, still standing, chimed in when I finished. While she prayed I peeked up at the men. Michael's lips were moving silently. Coy had a slightly pained look on his face. Not everybody "gets" that it's OK to pray for animals. In Jesus' day animals were valuable and you can bet that people prayed for their sick animals. By the time we finished our prayer, Daisy's paw was no longer bleeding. She moved away, limping slightly.

Daisy never forgot that prayer. During the six weeks of the School and on later visits, whenever she saw me she came over to me, tail wagging happily. If I squatted down, she'd lay her head on my knees with a deep sigh.

The four of us meandered down to the river, chatting away, getting to know each other better and planning the finer points of our jailbreak. We decided to go up to breakfast on Thursday to avoid suspicion. We would eat very lightly.

When we returned, I went to the small bookstore just off the classroom and found the two books that Sister Debbie recommended as well as another that caught my eye, *Recovery of the Inner Child.*

At 2:15 p.m. I met with Father Bernie and the other small group leaders in the coffee room.

"Because you said yes, God will help you," he said.

Like we could say no after you had already printed our names in the syllabus!

Each of the six of us had accepted the assignment of chairing our small discussion groups. Bernie asked us to help our group focus on each person's own journey; on our experience giving Spiritual Direction; on our personal experiences of things presented in the lectures and on current areas of personal difficulty.

He offered to be there for the leaders if we encountered any problems with our group.

Taking a deep breath and letting it out slowly, I headed downstairs to the library where we were assigned "the large table." Unfortunately the table was far away from the window. I will do anything to sit near a window and light!

Fortunately, there was no time for sorrow over this. My group members were arriving. There were five of us altogether.

We introduced ourselves briefly. I started off, to help put the group at ease.

Then Jack spoke; he was a married Catholic. He was tall and lanky with thinning hair; he always carried his porkpie hat, his defense against the sun.

Ann was an Episcopalian with one child. Ann was very active in the healing ministry in her home city. Her dark eyes crackled with intelligence.

Dick was a tall man with thinning hair. He was from a nearby state. He was also an Episcopalian. He and his wife had two children.

Costanzo was serving a term as the Vicar General of the Olivetan Benedictines. He lived at the Mother House in Siena, Italy. He was at Pecos to help the monastery solve a problem (the nature of which he never revealed to us). He had chosen to attend the School in connection with his ministry to the monastery.

Costanzo was a kind and humble man. He had served at a parish in Louisiana early in his pastorate. He was one of the only priests I have ever known who really liked women and what they care about. By this I mean that Ann and I could talk about our children and he would be genuinely interested. He was OK with tears. However, Costanzo had a few things to learn about Protestants. Today would be his first lesson.

I called the meeting to order and explained the possible tasks we had for our work together. I stressed the confidentiality of any personal disclosures.

I introduced an idea that was close to my heart, "I would like it if we could be an intercessory prayer group for each other while we are here. We can share confidential prayer requests with one another and pray for one another's prayer concerns."

Ann jumped right on it. She was in the prayer ministry in her home church and believed in the power of prayer to influence outcomes. Dick and Jack agreed. The idea of an intercessory prayer group was new to Costanzo. He knew a lot about praying for global concerns, but praying for our specific needs and intentions was new to him.

I decided to tell him a story of healing.

JoAnn and I were at the healing station, after the Eucharist. We were the assigned intercessors for private prayer after the service. A dear friend of ours came up for prayer. She would be having surgery in the morning for what was almost certainly cancer. Her surgeon had asked an oncologist, a cancer doctor, to be in the operating room to look at the tumor during surgery so he could see it with his own eyes. We agreed to pray for her and asked her if she would like to make her confession before surgery. We heard her confession. In the Episcopal Church, anyone can hear a confession.

When our friend went into surgery the next day, the sick organ had gone back to its normal size. Previously, the organ had been many times its normal size and, ominously, had had a fluid-filled cavity with a mass on a stalk in its center. The organ was removed and sent to pathology. That poor pathologist sliced that thing from end to end trying to find the tumor, but all the cells in the removed organ were normal. There was no longer a sac and no longer a stalked mass.

Costanzo could hardly contain himself.

"You heard her confession?" he asked, aghast.

"Anyone can hear a confession in the Episcopal Church."

Bewildered, Costanzo turned to Dick and Ann, the other two Episcopalians, to contradict me. Both confirmed that anyone in the Episcopal Church can hear a confession.

"Surely you did not give her ...," he choked out the last word, "absolution."

"Well, Father," I explained kindly, but firmly, "I do not know the effect of the absolution you give, but I was very pleased with the effect of mine."

He sat back in his chair, pale, stunned and bewildered. Dick and Ann continued to nod, smiling a bit to encourage and soothe him.

We agreed to become an intercessory prayer group for one another. Although I have detailed notes on the prayer requests, I promised my friends confidentiality, so I will simply say that each of us asked prayers for our own learning and healing in the School; each of us lifted up family members for healing. Costanzo entreated our prayers for a monk in Italy, part of his monastic community. Each of us promised to pray about Costanzo's mission to help the monastery.

I asked the group to think about our topic for the next session: "Why we do Spiritual Direction?" Then we broke for the day.

I invited Ann on a walk to the duck pond. As usual, I had graham crackers in my pocket. We fed the ducklings then we continued our walk, dodging puddles and circling the grounds. The grass in the middle of the track held some of last night's rain and wet the bottom of my khakis. We slipped into the chairs just as Vespers began, my wet pant legs clinging and cold against my legs.

More turkey for dinner, this time turkey meatballs with spaghetti. BA, Michael, Coy and I sat together again, this time joined by three of the monks. After dinner, we murmured together about our upcoming jailbreak on Thursday. We couldn't wait.

I wasn't able to call Sarah, as she was at the healing service with JoAnn.

Back in my room, missing my nightly talk with Sarah, I played the tape she had made for the day, then rewound and replayed the tapes she had made for me for the three days I had been there. I added the Tuesday photos she had sent to my collection on the wall.

I sat at my desk and began to read *Recovery of the Inner Child*. I was fascinated by a technique in the book. You hold a different colored pen in each hand. With your dominant hand, you write down a question and then answer it with your non-dominant hand. This gives you access to both the logical half of your brain and to the intuitive side of your brain.

Before long I was yawning. I crawled into bed with my prayer pig.

    peeking out
    from white robes
    the monk's sneakers

FOUR

1995, Pecos Benedictine Monastery, Week I, Wednesday

I pressed down the tiny switch on my travel alarm and put my feet on the floor, dreamily rejoicing in bugsong. I showered, then inspected the reddish brown handprint on my arm and realized that it would be with me for a long time. The one on my ribs was rapidly fading.

Just before six, I strode down the hall and took the road to the river. I stopped to feed the ducklings graham crackers then followed the river road and the trail to the waterfall. I paused to watch a tiny dam of grass and sticks beside the woodland path. Every few moments the water behind the four-inch dam would rush out, then the dam would refill. *When water is troubled, God is healing something.*

I circled back to the residence returning to my room with just enough time to clean the mud off of my sneakers and to slip on my Birkenstocks.

With only seconds to spare before the Eucharist began, I slid into a chair beside BA and Michael. Praise songs lifted me up.

Breakfast was the same wonderful smorgasbord. Sister Judith, a tiny, thirty-something nun from the Community, joined the four of us at table.

I had selected a banana as part of my meal. I proceeded to slice the unpeeled banana lengthwise and to sprinkle the cut surfaces with brown sugar. I scooped each bite out of the peel with a spoon.

'Are you an Episcopal nun?' Judith asked huffily. *Way too much emotion. I wonder what this is about?* I asked her to say more. In her training as a nun, she had been taught to eat fruit without touching it and my handling of the banana made her think of that. Her novice mistress, she said, was a woman who was a bit hard to enjoy.

"I learned this from my pastor's wife," I explained. "It is even better with lime juice squeezed on it before the brown sugar."

Judith told me that she wanted to get to know me better. We agreed to meet in my room that afternoon after my Physical Wellness class.

After breakfast I settled into my sunbeam. I picked up my stitching, my notebook open on the chair beside me. Abbot David was to give us a third lecture on the Charismatic Renewal. I had the most wonderful, non-verbal bond with Abbot David. He was always saying things that I was already thinking and it was a real blessing to hear these things come out of someone else's mouth. I don't think that we had a single conversation, but I felt so connected to him. *Thought-buddies.*

He spoke of the sacraments as a place where people with great differences could gather and join in one celebration. He praised religious studies, but insisted that it was essential to put it all back together after study and to worship and serve, informed by that study.

"Your actions reveal more about what you believe than your words or thoughts."

"Teach by example."

Abbot David said that the ultimate credential was anointing by the Holy Spirit.

Oh, David, I am not so sure of that; I know some real jerks that speak in tongues.

I remembered what my teacher, Dr. Karl Menninger, had said, "If you analyze a jerk, you get an analyzed jerk." I knew a few people baptized in the Spirit who never produce the fruits of the Holy Spirit: love, joy, peace, patience, kindness, goodness, faithfulness, gentleness and self control.

Maybe if you baptize a jerk in the Holy Spirit, you get a jerk baptized in the Holy Spirit.

After class we had a break. The class spilled out through the heavy wooden doors onto the hard packed dirt driveway. BA and I sat down near the hollyhocks, to the right of the door.

"Have you ever seen a hollyhock wedding? " she asked. I shook my head. She produced four toothpicks from the pocket of her white skirt and proceeded to make a bride out of a white hollyhock blossom. The upside down flower became the skirt and two buds became the torso and head, all joined together by a toothpick. Then she made three bridesmaids, one with a skirt of palest pink, the next with a skirt of medium pink and the third with a skirt of hot pink.

I held them gently against my heart as I carried them back inside. I set them on the seat beside me, next to my notebook.

After the next lecture, I carried the hollyhock wedding to my room, where I placed it on wet paper towels on my Formica desk, in the hope of keeping it fresh. I hurried to the dining room to join my friends.

BA was already sitting with Michael and Coy. She was wearing a hot pink hollyhock behind her right ear. Lunch was turkey spaghetti sauce and pasta, with a side salad. The four of us just grinned at each other. No words about the jailbreak tomorrow were necessary. I took an orange from the big bowl of fruit that was always available. I peeled it with my hands, lest anyone else think I was a nun.

After lunch, BA and I visited the gift shop, browsing companionably, but not buying anything. After returning the key to the welcome desk, we circled the grounds in a leisurely way that accommodated our lively conversation.

Soon it was time for Physical Wellness. Most of my classmates were already in the classroom waiting for Brother Matt. He showed up right on time. We followed him to the gym. My heart fluttering in trepidation, I took a place in the very back row, in the corner. My tall friend, Coy, exercised beside me.

Our leader, Brother Matt had a fitness training certificate from The Aerobics Research Institute. There are eight kinds of intelligence, one being Physical; Physical Intelligence comes in last on my personal list.

I could not follow Matt's instructions quickly. I did my best, but when he called a break after 45 minutes, I left, with a quiet wave to Coy.

I went back to my room. Physical stamina was not the issue, trying to follow his instructions was emotionally draining for me. This was worsened by shame since my classmates followed him with little effort.

Waiting for my appointment with Judith, I read some more in *Recovery of the Inner Child.*

Soon enough I heard Judith tapping lightly on my door. I invited her in. Her eyes immediately went to my collection of photos on the wall.

"You are not supposed to put anything on the wall!"

Catholics can be so unthinking about rules!

"Judith, I am a homeowner. I would not do anything to hurt the walls."

She relaxed.

She shared a little about her adventures in religious life. I asked about this "daily crucifixion of community life." She explained that there are always a few Community members who are hard to enjoy, and a few who are very hard to enjoy.

I told her a little about my work, my marriage, my daughter and my hopes for healing while I was there.

"Costanzo was very upset when he returned to the Cloister on Tuesday," she said. "He was distraught that his small group was led by a fallen Catholic."

I was taken aback. *Oh, Costanzo, I didn't fall, I was pushed!*

I found it astonishing that anyone could characterize someone with as lively and deep a faith as mine as "fallen."

We chatted a while longer and agreed to meet again.

I called Sarah. She was feeling great! She had enjoyed the healing service. She was reading my letters every day. I told her that I was playing and replaying her tapes to me, and I was putting the pictures she sent up on the wall. I prayed with her about her back. She has scoliosis and had to wear a brace every night. She thanked me and we hung up.

My call to the healing ministry had come when she was seven, six weeks before she was diagnosed with scoliosis. By the time the diagnosis was made, I was already taking a class in praying for healing.

Dinner was turkey sloppy joes and salad. I couldn't wait for our jailbreak. As we walked downstairs, I asked Coy if he wanted to walk in the mornings at six. He declined, saying that his walking time was late afternoon.

Later I asked Michael. He was game! He promised to ask community members about alternate walking trails nearby. The Community still regarded Michael as Benedictine and thus as a brother. Michael and I agreed to meet at the grandfather clock outside the chapel at 6 o'clock in the morning.

At the healing service, Abbot David first led us through a renewal of our Baptism and Confirmation vows. I was very familiar with this. We did this five times a year in the Episcopal Church.

I was eager to ask for prayer for the gift of forgiveness. I had prayed daily for this grace. I had fasted. I had asked my friends to pray with me for the gift to forgive two people in my life who were hurtful. All to no avail. I also wanted to ask for the perceived infilling of the Holy Spirit, the experience of joy.

I went up and stated my requests. Abbot Andrew, assisted by several community members, prayed for me for a time. I felt nothing. I prayed in tongues. Nothing. I prayed in English. "Please help me to forgive. I will go anywhere. I will do anything." Nothing.

Abbot Andrew asked if I had gotten what I wanted. I said that I had not. He continued to pray for me. Abbot David came over and told him to move on.

So much for thought-buddies!

Abbot Andrew didn't give up. Finally the forgiveness came. I was free. I felt no joy but I was delighted with the forgiveness and I thanked the Abbot for not giving up on me.

I returned to my room after the service and curled up on top of the covers, hugging my knees. I felt like every cell in my body had been scrubbed clean.

After an hour, I put on my pajamas, crawled under the covers and fell fast asleep.

At 3 a.m., I awakened. Something was different. It took me a moment to figure out what was different. I no longer felt the resentment that I had always felt at having to come back to this world from heaven!

I began to praise God. "Thank you, Jesus!" I said again and again.

Suddenly I was flooded with joy. I felt that I had been caught up in a flash flood, a wonderful flash flood that tumbled me head over heels, spinning me into a torrent of each of the rainbow hues of joy.

I laid there for an hour reveling in the joy, and then drifted into a dreamless sleep.

FAX to Costanzo
I didn't fall
I was pushed

FIVE

1995, Pecos Benedictine Monastery, Week I, Thursday

I awakened before my alarm sounded. Little jolts of ecstasy still bubbled in my veins, as if my blood vessels were filled with ginger ale. I experienced anew the freedom of forgiveness. And I experienced the new freedom of being "OK" with having to come back here after visiting heaven. The bubbles of joy doubled my enjoyment of bugsong.

6:00 a. m., Michael, the perfect monastic, was right on time.

True to his word, Michael had inquired of the monks and learned of a good hiking trail, a jeep trail across the road from the monastery.

The heavy wooden door creaked loudly in the cold air as we pushed it open. We stepped outside onto the hard-packed yellow-orange earth of the driveway. As we walked up to the gate the thermometer on my jacket zipper registered fifty degrees. We crossed State Highway 63 and we walked several hundred feet to the right.

The jeep trail made a sharp left as it zigged obliquely up the mountain. It was one and a half lanes wide, just wide enough for two vehicles to pass one another cautiously.

The road was strewn with splintered rock created when the road was cut. Sharp rocks one inch to four inches in diameter obligated mindful placement of our feet. The rock was the same yellow-orange as the dirt in the monastery driveway.

As we moved uphill, we passed a cattle gate on our right. We saw a house beyond the gate and heard the barking of the ranch dogs upset about our approach. We followed the jeep trail, ever ascending to the left.

Breathless on the steep trail, we each pretended to be praying.

At the farthest ascent allowed by our schedule was a pine, right on the fence line. Over the years, three strands of barbed wire had grown into its heartwood. Every time a gust of wind moved the pine and stretched the barbed wire, I could hear an eerie moaning sound. I felt like barbed wire had grown into my heartwood, too.

The healing the night before had removed one strand of barbed wire. I hoped that more strands would come out as the School unfolded. We paused to catch our breath. I looked up. I could see the waning crescent moon right overhead. *God's thumbnail.* We turned back towards the monastery that was becoming home to us.

Now that we had the breath for talking, we chattered away. I told Michael stories about my big Irish-German family and my adventures to date in life. I shared what had happened to me the night before. Michael was happy that I had received the rest of the Baptism in the Holy Spirit.

He then told stories about his family, the food they made and, even more interestingly, stories about the monastery where he lived for 17 years, Christ in the Desert, near Abiquiu, New Mexico.

We made much better time going downhill, arriving back before the bell for morning worship. I returned to my room and slipped off my sneakers, replacing them with my Birks just as the bell sounded. BA was already waiting in the chairs. Michael joined us soon after.

The Abbot introduced a twist to the sermon that was new to the School members: open mike time. He gave a very brief homily and then invited members of the School to come to the microphone and speak as they were led.

He smiled as he told us that sweaty palms were an infallible sign the Holy Spirit was calling us to speak. There must not have been any sweaty palms because none of us went up to the mike that day.

At breakfast, Michael, Coy and BA got coffee and sat down together at an empty octagonal table. Each wore a secret smile. I took a banana and some brown sugar to make a nun-such banana and joined them, grinning.

Prescient, the Abbot sat down quietly with us. Michael, wise in the ways of dealing with Benedictine superiors, instantly adopted a bland, unreadable face. So did Coy. Perhaps superiors in the Disciples of Christ must be handled in the same way as Benedictine superiors. BA and I exchanged a merry glance. The Abbot watched with interest as I prepared my banana and spooned it up. With a twinkle in his eye, he observed that Michael, Coy and BA were not eating much. The Abbot finished his cereal and left the room.

We burst into nervous giggles. *Like a monk, a preacher, a white-haired lady and a doctor are going to get into trouble during a jailbreak.*

The others took a few moments to finish their coffee, wanting to give the Abbot plenty of time to get back to his room, near where Coy's car was parked.

We retired briefly to our rooms. I went outside and met Coy and the others at his car. We whispered, aware of the Abbot's nearby presence in his room.

It was already warmer, sixty degrees. The sky was a beautiful cloudless deep blue. BA and I hopped into the back seat of the car.

After ten miles on winding two-lane highways, we were on Interstate 25, headed toward Santa Fe. After a short ride, we turned onto the Old Las Vegas (New Mexico) Highway, which forms a north access road to I-25.

After several miles we crunched into the dirt and gravel parking lot of Harry's Roadhouse. We saw an infallible sign of fine food: the lot was filled with pickups and BMWs. Harry's was a low-slung, white-painted house, decorated with swirls of turquoise and magenta. The door and doorframe were a deep turquoise. Yellow daisies and silver Dusty Miller spilled out of a weathered half-barrel by the front door.

The small square entryway was floored with concrete. The turquoise-painted doors to the ladies and men's rooms were straight ahead as we entered. Before turning right into the restaurant, we stopped to peer at a huge bulletin board covered in announcements of local art shows, baby sitters, and horses for sale. We stepped into a small indoor eating area with a few red leatherette booths and tiny kitchenette tables. Handmade pies and cakes filled glass shelves against the back window.

We stepped outside into the rapidly warming air and grabbed the first table near the door, under a trellis. The outside dining area was a magical "room" where bees and hummingbirds hovered over annuals and perennials. I positioned myself against the wall of the house so that I could watch the hummers as they moved from plant to plant. It was now a delightful seventy degrees with a light breeze. I slipped off my jacket.

The owner, a tall, slender, dark-haired man with wavy hair gathered into a ponytail, came to take our beverage orders. Fresh squeezed orange juice all around. Soon he was back, our glasses clinking against one another on his tray.

He whipped a pad from a pocket in his apron. "May I take your order?"

"'Can you bring us some cholesterol?" I said.

"That can be arranged," he said smoothly. The twinkle in his eye looked a lot like the one I'd seen in the Abbot's eye.

I wonder how many refugees he gets from the monastery.

I ordered migas: scrambled eggs with sautéed onions, roasted Hatch pepper strips, fresh tomatoes, and deep fried tortilla strips, accompanied by refried beans and warm flour tortillas. The migas was soft, savory, and crunchy at once. Divine.

By the time we finished breakfast, the day waitress had arrived. She crouched beside the table and told us about the desserts. Devil's food cake, red velvet cake, carrot cake, cherry pie, apple raisin pie, coconut cream pie, and lemon meringue pie. A tongue stud gleamed in her mouth. White-haired BA was so undone by the tongue stud that the waitress had to repeat the dessert menu for her.

I ordered cherry pie with ice cream and two orders of coconut cream pie to go. One for me and one for Carole. The others also ordered an extra dessert to go.

My cherry pie was wrapped in a flaky crust and filled with abundant tart cherries. The ice cream was superlatively high fat and made a wonderful contrast to the cherries.

After dessert we lingered, talking, sharing our lives, discussing the School and our goals for our time there.

I have three good friends and a reliable source for cholesterol. Now I can go deep.

Aloud, I said, "It is only the fifth day, but I have already received almost all of the healings I had hoped for when I came here. I cannot wait to see what God is going to do next. This afternoon I will work with a two-handed writing technique I read about in *Recovery of Your Inner Child,* which I bought in the bookstore."

BA was enthusiastic: "We used that book in the rehab where I worked as a psychiatric aide. The patients loved it."

The men showed polite interest in my plans.

I guess this technique is "girl stuff."

As we drove back toward the monastery along the Las Vegas Highway, Michael directed us to watch for a tiny Hispanic church on our left. We found it by going straight after the Highway plunged under I-25.

We parked under an ancient tree. The church's front door was right up against the road. The church itself was built deep into the steep hillside, against the summer heat. We started to head up the hill.

"Watch for rattlesnakes!" Michael called.

Rattlesnakes! I didn't sign up for rattlesnakes.

Now watching every step, we climbed the small hill. We each went to a window and held our hands beside our eyes, pressing our faces to the clear glass. A dozen feet below me was the floor of the church. There were 15 pews and a center aisle. The walls were a creamy pale yellow. The only decorations were a crucifix above the altar and simple Stations of the Cross.

Mindful of the containers of cream pie in the car, we did not stay long. We vowed to return and explore the graveyard with its handmade gravestones on another day.

Driving through Glorieta on our way back to the monastery, BA and I spied a sign, "Good Food" with "Renate's European

Restaurant" in smaller letters. We looked at each other and smiled. We knew that we would be visiting Renate's. Very soon. We were sure that we could persuade the guys to come along, which would be essential since Coy had the only car among the four of us.

Our laughter rose as we approached the monastery. We had been glad to leave. Glad to have a break from turkey. But we were glad to be home again.

I went to my room and opened the curtains to let in more natural light. I put the two servings of pie on the dresser for later. I reviewed the instructions in *Recovery of the Inner Child* and selected a purple pen for my right hand and a green one for my left.

Because I am right handed, my left hand is controlled by my right brain, which is my intuitive, creative brain.

The dialogue between my right hand/ left-brained self and my left hand/ right-brained self follows. The logical right-handed questions and comments are labeled "Me" and the intuitive left-handed responses are labeled "Little me." "Little me" usually speaks in the voice of a little child, so the grammar and syntax are imperfect. I have made no attempt to edit "Little me's" grammar. Here is what my two hands wrote:

Me: Hello, I love you; I'd like to know you better.

Little me: I love you too.

Me: I'm big. Tell me about yourself.

Little me: I'm small. I'm smart, though.

Me: Smart. I believe that. I can see it in your eyes.

Little me: Raisin eyes.

Me: Raisin eyes. You are a poet!

Little me: Yes, I am.

Me: Do you have a poem?

Little me: I do.

Me: Tell me.

48

Little me: *Roses are blue*
                And so are you

Me: Well, that is for sure. I am thinking about so many things. And I miss Sarah.

Little me: I like Sarah. She plays with me.

Me: She does! I have disappointed her by my fear of playing. You too, I suppose?

Little me: That's for sure!

Me: What do you want to play?

Little me: I want to play ball.

Me: Ball. Would Koosh be ok??

Little me: Yes. I like your juggle balls, too.

Me: You like my juggle balls. I do, too. But they scare me.

Little me: I feel afraid sometimes, but I like to juggle.

Me: I'm glad you like to juggle. What makes you afraid?

Little me: Noise. Angry God people.

Me: Angry God people? Tell me about them.

Little me: Big Nun and Big Priest.

Me: Big Nun and Big Priest scare you?

Little me: Yes!

Me: Can you say what you fear?

Little me: Hurt me. Tell me shut up.

Me: You are afraid that they will hurt you or tell you to shut up?

Little me: Yes. Hit me or not listen.

Me: Big Nun or Big Priest might hit you or not listen to you.

Little me: Yes.

Me: I won't let them hit you.

Little me: Good!

Me: Do you trust me to protect you from hitting?

Little me: Yes. I suppose.

Me: You sort of trust me to keep them from hitting you?

Little me: Yes.

Me: Do you trust me enough go near them?

Little me: I don't want to.

Me: You would prefer not to?

Little me: Yes.

Me: What would make you feel safe?

Little me: A little close.

Me: You'd try it a little?

Little me: Yes.

Me: Ok. What about talking?

Little me: They not like Jesus.

Me: Do you know Jesus?

Little me: Yes.

Me: Do you like Him?

Little me: Yes.

Me: What do you like about Him?

Little me: He nice. He no hurt me.

Me: Jesus doesn't hurt you?

Little me: No.

Me: Is there something you want to teach Big Nun or Big Priest?

Little me: Be like Jesus.

Me: What is Jesus like?

Little me: Nice. Quiet. No yelling.

Me: Jesus is nice, quiet and doesn't yell?

Little me: Yes.

Me: Anything else?

Little me: He loves me.

Me: Jesus loves you?

Little me: Yes.

Me: But Big Nun and Big Priest don't?

Little me: No! They think they know everything.

Me: They don't love you and they think they know everything?

Little me: Right!

Me: Do you think they need more love?

Little me: Yes.

Me: How can they get it?

Little me: I can give them some of the love Jesus gave me.

Me: You can give them some of the love Jesus gave you?

Little me: Yes.

Me: How?

Little me: Raisin eyes. Smile.

Me: You can send love through your eyes and your smile.

Little me: Yes.

Me: Is it true that you don't feel safe talking to them right now?

Little me: Yes.

Me: OK.

I finished writing and reread what my right and left hands had written. The left-handed writing was rather messy. But as I read it the hairs on my neck stood up.

The youthful, playful part of me is filled with wisdom and compassion! And she knows Jesus. I want to get to know her better! And to take advantage of her wisdom.

And I am long overdue for spending time with my juggle balls.

I glanced at my clock. Time to meet Carole. I grabbed the two slices of pie and two white plastic forks and headed around the corner to Carole's room. She invited me in.

We dove into our pie, the only sound little groans of pleasure. The meringue was soft and tender. The filling was very coconut-y but the strands of coconut had been removed, so the whole impression was of cool smoothness.

With a final groan, we laid our forks inside of our pie containers and set about getting to know each other better.

I was eager to hear about Carole's Near Death Experience (NDE), which occurred during a surgical procedure. She asked about my NDE.

We talked of our relationships with our mutual friend Sheila and the work each of us does in the healing ministry.

Carole showed me the quilt she was working on, which was a beautiful blend of red, white and blue. I helped her with the binding, which was giving her trouble. I thanked her again for her care the morning of Sarah's surgery. *Was that only yesterday?* We bade each other goodbye, promising to meet again.

There was 30 minutes before afternoon chapel, so I went around the corner to my room and grabbed two of my juggle balls. They are made of salmon-colored oilcloth and filled with millet seed. One has a mended spot from when a mouse became interested in the millet seed.

I headed out the door nearest to my room and walked along the road to the orchard. I tossed the juggle balls from hand to hand, trying to keep both moving at once. I didn't do too badly, though I dropped one from time to time. As I approached the orchard, I saw three immature windfall apples in the road, each tinged with pink. *Maybe someone else has been juggling!*

The bell calling us to Vespers rang. I headed back, leaving the juggle balls in my room. In the chapel I nodded to Coy, who sat alone at the end of our row and joined Michael and BA further down the row, near the Guadalupe mural.

Dinner was turkey Salisbury steak, which didn't seem so bad now that we knew we could have a break from it any time we wanted.

After dinner, I spoke to Sarah and prayed with her for her back. Then the class had a videotape on the life and work of Carl Jung. I watched it with polite interest. I was trained as a Freudian and the Jungian concepts never really click with me. I knew that I would have a lot of time that I could use my hands for stitching, not writing.

Always an introvert, I slipped away from the others after the film. I followed the long corridor and turned right at the corridor that went in front of Carole's room. When I got to my corner, I turned left marveling at the golden tan walls of the corridor. The walls, doors and windows were curved at the edges as if they were made of adobe. I walked halfway along the corridor to my room.

I listened to the tape Sarah had made for the day and mounted today's photos on the wall over my desk.

I reread my inner dialog. Once again the hairs on my neck stood up. *I need to do more of these dialogs! This little kid knows things!* I crawled into bed and fell into a deep sleep.

three strands of barbed wire
grown into its heartwood
the moaning pine

53

SIX

1995, Pecos Benedictine Monastery, Week I, Friday

I awakened with my alarm. Bugsong was in full chorus. I lay there for a moment marveling at my good fortune to be on this mountain. And to be free of the unforgiveness that had plagued me for so many years. My heart sang with happiness and gratitude. I showered, checking the handprints. The one on my ribs was faded nearly completely. The one on my arm was now tanned to a reddish brown. *Battle stripes.* I got ready for the day and hurried down the hall.

Michael was waiting for me. We set out for the jeep trail, chatting happily until we reached the trail. Then we were silent, focusing on breathing as we climbed the mountain. When we reached the moaning pine, we paused for several minutes to catch our breath, and then turned back. On the way down the mountain, we talked of yesterday's adventure to Harry's and the tiny buried-in-the-hillside church with its purple-orange soil. We were both looking forward to more adventures away from the monastery.

Not too many adventures, I hope, I have come here to go deep, to be healed.

Back at the monastery, we parted. I returned to my room. I slipped off my athletic shoes and slid my feet into my sandals. The bell rang and I hurried down the hall to the chapel.

The Praise songs lifted me up into joy.

Two classmates braver than me spoke at open-mike time.

I breakfasted with my three friends. The feeling at breakfast this day was warm and enjoyable, without the tension of the previous day. I was so thankful to have found three good friends with whom to share meals, walks and other adventures. I looked around. Other groups of three or four kindred spirits had found one another. The Abbot was visiting with one group of three, smiling and joking. I laughed to think of how tense we'd been yesterday morning when he sat with us just before our jailbreak.

After breakfast, we moved downstairs to the classroom.

The overhead lights were off. We each took our accustomed places, me in the back row, against the windows, right of center; Michael a few rows in front of me at the end of the aisle; Coy near the center of the room; BA in the row behind, one seat to the right of our tall friend Coy, so that she could see.

Sister Theresa, our lecturer for the morning, was standing quietly in the right front of the room, holding a framed rectangular picture against her chest.

Theresa was a tall, somber nun from Nebraska. Her black wavy hair had a blaze of white on the right side. She had taught Special Education students for ten years before entering the convent. Compassion, patience and stillness were etched onto her face.

Theresa stood waiting until we quieted.

"Each of you is a gift to the world."

She moved to the person in the rightmost seat in the front row and unfolded her arms, revealing that she had been holding a mirror to her chest. The mirror's surface was overprinted with the image of Jesus from the Shroud of Turin. She held the mirror up to the woman so that she could see her own face in the mirror, with Jesus' face overlying it. Theresa began to speak soothingly, using her teacher's voice so that all could hear her words.

"You are God's gift to the world. Sometimes gifts are plain, sometimes gifts are beautiful. Sometimes gifts get damaged in the mail and are a little worse for the wear. None of this matters. You are God's gift to this world. He gave you unique gifts, gifts of His Own traits, so that you can reflect who He is to the world. Let your gifts shine forth. Be who He made you to be. Bless us with who you are."

The woman burst into tears before Theresa's second sentence was finished. By the time Theresa got to the second woman quiet sounds of thirty three people sobbing filled the room. Each of us had reached for the box of Kleenex under our chair and placed it in our lap.

As Theresa finished with each person, she reached into the pocket of her oversized sweater and pulled out a three-inch heart that she had cut from red construction paper. Theresa had glued a one inch square of mirror to the center of each heart. She handed the heart to the person she had just blessed, and moved on to the next.

Theresa moved through the room, holding up the mirror for each of us. Her words were like a free verse lullaby, different for each of us, yet always touching the same themes.

Everyone sitting in the rows behind where Theresa was working watched her intently. Everyone in the room listened to every word that Theresa spoke. No one moved except to take more Kleenex.

Theresa approached me in my back row seat. My eyes were already swollen and red. I looked into the mirror, past the beloved face of Jesus at my own and listened to her words, struggling to embrace them. Deep in my soul, I knew that her words were true. I also knew that it would take a lot of healing before I could fully embrace the message I was a gift to this world. Finishing with me, Theresa handed me my mirrored heart. I could already imagine it taped to the front of my red spiral notebook, so that I would see it every day and remember her blessing.

Theresa walked quietly to the front of the room. She looked at each of us intently, checking to see if we were OK.

"You might want to sit here a few minutes to absorb your impressions of these moments. When you are ready, you may take a break."

She paused for a moment and moved through the curtained French doors to the cloister.

We all stayed seated in the dimmed room. The occasional sniffle and muffled sob could still be heard. Finally one of the more vigorous men arose and pushed open one of the dove-carved wooden doors, flooding the room with sunlight. He went outside. One by one the rest of us moved outside. We were a subdued group during that break, talking quietly in small groups of two or three. Some of us still clutched wads of Kleenex. Some of us, including me, had eyes that were still leaking.

Ann came up to me quietly and suggested a walk in the afternoon. I quickly agreed. She walked away. I went back to my Kleenex.

Theresa had placed a plastic trashcan outside the doors to collect our Kleenex before we returned to the classroom. Slowly, one by one, we returned inside. I tossed in my Kleenex, confident I had a whole box under my chair and a cloth handkerchief in each of my pockets.

That will be a hard act to follow!

The lights were back on and Abbot Andrew was waiting for us, with a kind smile on his face. As he began to speak of using Scripture to help Spiritual Directees as they walked with God, the occasional sob or sniffle still could be heard.

It was a morning for remarkable kindness. In the midst of his talk, a woman who sat near the front raised her hand and asked him if he could provide a list of Scripture verses to give to directees in various situations. Probably I was the only one in the room to notice his tiny twitch of shock and dismay. He kept a very straight face and a very kind voice in responding.

"The best way to know what verses to apply will be your own ongoing deep study of the Scriptures. With this knowledge base, the Holy Spirit can more easily show you Scriptures to suggest to your directees."

Duh, I thought, in a tone less kindly than the Abbot's.

The Benedictine Rule requires the monks to treat guests as if they were Christ himself. The Abbot stepped up to the plate. I am glad to report that within three days, he had created the list she asked for and handed it to all of us.

Thankfully the Abbot dismissed us early. I, for one, was mentally exhausted from the joyful weeping. I wanted to wash my face and to lie down for a bit before lunch.

In my room I lay down and closed my eyes. I fell immediately into a deep sleep. The lunch bell startled me awake. I washed my face again and hurried down the hall and climbed the steps to the lunchroom.

I took a turkey burger and salad and joined my dear friends at one of the octagonal tables. BA and I still had red eyes. The men were subdued but stoic. We ate in near silence.

I returned to my room. *Thank goodness we have the afternoon off.*

I climbed onto my bed, back against the wall, and started reading Henri Nouwen's *Beyond the Mirror.* This short book is an account of Henri's Near Death Experience and his life afterwards. Walking beside the road one icy morning, Nouwen was struck by the mirror of a van. He suffered a ruptured spleen and lay near death in the ICU for several days while he waited for an Operating Room to free up. He described how easy it was to be kind and compassionate when hovering at Heaven's door and how very difficult it was to stay in that place of kindness, compassion and non-judgmental-ness when he was well again. *That's for sure!*

When I was on the ceiling, during my own NDE, observing the doctor's wrong-headed remark, I did not judge him, but felt compassion for him. How hard it is for me, back in the flesh, to avoid judging. When someone "'hurts me'" I experience a constellation of body sensations that recurs whenever I think of the "hurt." Even today, I struggle to grasp the spiritual truth that if I avoided saying, "he shouldn't have done that," I wouldn't be "hurt." Instead I'd be free. I am pretty sure that I will spend the rest of my life in the flesh struggling with this tendency to hold on to hurts.

Beyond the mirror. I thought of a Dallas restaurant that I had visited. Every surface of the ladies' room was mirrored, even the wall behind the toilet. Those mirrors were about "me, me, me." Theresa's mirror and Henri's mirror reminded me of how different a mirror can be if it reflects not just me, but the face and heart of Jesus.

I began to think of my relationship with Jesus. Unfortunately we had not always been friends. After my faith was stolen, I got back the Father/Creator first, then the Spirit. It would be years before I could become comfortable with Jesus.

I lay down and took a nap. I was still exhausted. Soon my alarm chirped and I was off to meet Ann for a walk before chapel. Her room was on the long corridor that ran the length of the monastery from the classroom to the exit to the nuns' dormitory. I looked out the window at the river as I approached her door. We exited the river door and headed for the dirt road leading to the duck pond.

We fed the ducks then sat on a bench near the duck pond. We saw Coy walking and reading at the same time. *Brave.* We shared deeply about our faith and our work in the healing ministry. Soon, too soon, the bell rang, calling us to chapel and dinner afterwards.

Ann joined me in sitting with my three friends at dinner. Turkey spaghetti again. Thankfully, turkey spaghetti sauce is hard to tell from the "regular."

After dinner I went to the snack room and called Sarah. We prayed together on the phone for healing of her back. The x-rays had been ominous recently, with ever-increasing spinal curves. Both were now up to 65 degrees. The doctors were watching the growth plates in her back, ready to do surgery when the growth plates closed. Neither Sarah nor I liked the idea of fusing eleven of her vertebrae together into one.

The evening lecture was a short one. Father Paul passed out the Myers-Briggs Inventories. He asked us to fill them out and return them in the morning. He spoke briefly about the personality typology that would be revealed by the test. He dismissed us and encouraged us to return to our rooms and fill them out.

I had taken this test several times before. I always struggled with it. You had to choose between one of two items for each question. I was always saying to myself, *but, but, I like them both,* when I filled it out. For me there were no clear-cut choices. I sat at my desk, sighed and filled it out. I still struggled to pick my favorite one of the pairs.

I returned to my room where I journaled and re-read parts of Henri Nouwen's book. I played Sarah's tape for the day and posted two more pictures to the wall. I turned in early and fell into an exhausted sleep.

cool morning
hugging clothes
warm from the dryer

SEVEN

1995, Pecos Benedictine Monastery, Week I, Saturday

Saturday at six a.m. Michael and I hiked up the mountain. We got back at just before seven. Michael returned to his room.

I slipped into a small consultation room off of the chapel where the monastic community was having a private Eucharist. The School's Eucharist would be at 3 p.m. I closed the door softly and approached a small mosaic of bread and wine mounted on the wall against the chapel. Placing a hand on either side of the mosaic, I began to pray for the community. I prayed until I heard them finish, then quietly left the small room and followed the main hallway to the classroom.

I sat in my seat and leaned back to study the ceiling. Massive lodge pole pine beams, dark and shiny, traversed the ceiling from the fireplace to the window wall. Creamy white plaster filled in between the logs.

I heard the voices and footfalls of my classmates coming down the long hallway. When they arrived, I stood and joined them at the base of the stairs to the dining room. When the bell rang, we trooped upstairs.

I always ascended the stairs to the left so I could touch the bluntly carved point of the lodge pole pine upright at the turn of the stairs. Today I also trailed my fingers along the cold, heavy iron chain that formed a stair rail for the upper stairs.

The breakfast buffet was arrayed on two cafeteria tables aligned with the long axis of the room. Multi-gallon containers of several varieties of cereal, as well as huge containers of oat bran and wheat bran covered the near end. Bowls of nuts, sunflower seeds and raisins came next and then bowls of fruit. The milk dispensers, coffee and tea were in the right rear corner of the room.

After heaping a bowl with rolled oats, oat bran, slivered almonds and raisins, I covered the cereal with whole milk and joined my breakfast buddies. We were in fine fettle that morning. We had most of the day off the next day, Sunday, and had planned another outing to Harry's for breakfast and then on to the museums on the square in downtown Santa Fe. We planned to stop at Renate's for lunch on the way back.

After breakfast, we took our places in the classroom. Sr. Geralyn spoke to us about Prayer and Creative Movement (Dance). The more she talked the more I panicked. Coordinated movement, especially movement when another can see me, causes me great anxiety. I was not looking forward to this activity, scheduled for the coming week.

Father Paul followed with a lecture on the life cycle. I liked Paul. Like I did with Abbot David, I felt in a "mind meld" with Fr. Paul when he was lecturing. I often anticipated his next sentence. We hardly ever talked one to one, but I saw him as a "thought buddy."

After class, I had 45 minutes until lunch. I hurried back to my room to do a right- hand/ left-hand dialog to explore my anxiety about Creative Movement.

Again I selected purple ink for my right hand and lime green for my left:

How do you feel about this dance business?

Scared.

You feel frightened?

Yes!

What are you afraid would happen?

Cry. Not stop.

You are afraid you will cry and not stop?

Yes.

You would cry all day?

Yes.

Then what?

Don't know. Not stop.

Do you think you would cry for one hour?

Well, I suppose not.

So you would eventually stop crying?

Yes. Feels like forever though.

So it feels like you would cry and cry and not be able to stop, but probably you would stop?

Yes.

So, is there something else about starting to cry that bothers you?

People see.

You don't like that people see you crying and not stopping?

Don't like people see. Don't like people think I bad because I cry.

It is painful for you to imagine that they think you are bad because you cry?

Yes. They think I'm not OK or crazy.

You believe that they think you are coming unglued or going crazy?

Yes.

Do you feel like that when you cry so hard?

I do feel like my body is coming apart.

You feel like your body is dissolving?

Yes. Around eyes. Upper arms.

You feel like the parts around your eyes and your upper arms are dissolving?

Yes.

Babies feel like their bodies are dissolving when they feel pain. Do you feel like a baby?

Yes.

Do you think you would really dissolve?

No.

Can I ask you about something else?

Yes.

Would you try the movement stuff?

Yes.

OK

The bell for lunch had long since rung. I ran down the hall without rereading the dialog.

I dashed up the stairs. I served myself some oriental turkey salad with crisp noodles and sat down with my buddies. The turkey salad was rather good. Its goodness did not prevent us from fantasizing about our breakfast at Harry's in the morning or our later lunch at Renate's.

After lunch I returned to my room and read the dialog above. I saw that the dialog has served to reassure and realign the fearful part of me so that I was free to make an informed choice about trying Geralyn's Sacred Dance class.

I wanted to dialog about Physical Wellness. I agreed with the principle of it, but did not enjoy it in the least. I enjoyed my walks on the grounds and the morning hikes up the mountain, but I wasn't so sure about Physical Wellness. I planned to revisit the Sacred Dance issue to make sure that I was OK with it.

I chose purple and green pens again. Note: the dialog centers on a monk I shall call Xavier because his name is not Xavier.

What are you feeling?

I am scared

You are feeling scared?

Yes.

What is frightening you?

Xavier.

Xavier scares you?

Yes, Xavier scared, too. And sad.

Xavier is scared and he is sad?

Yes.

So sad scared Xavier frightens you?

Yes.

What are you afraid of?

No play. Hurt.

You are afraid that instead of playing and having fun, sad scared Xavier will hurt you?

Yes.

What can we do?

Love Xavier. Pray. Smile.

We can love him by praying for him, and smiling at him?

Yes.

What shall we pray for?

Peace. Love. Joy.

We should pray for peace, love and joy for sad scared Xavier?

Happy, brave X.

So we will pray for peace, love and joy for happy, brave Xavier.

Yes.

Are you OK with calisthenics and the sacred dance?

Dance.

No calisthenics?

No. Yuck. Not afraid. Just yuck.

OK, we won't do Physical Wellness again. Are you OK with juggling?

OK. Slow.

I'll go slow.

OK.

I grabbed two juggle balls and headed out the side door and down the dirt road toward the apple orchard. I tossed them back and forth slowly for the most part keeping both in motion at all times. I was getting better at it.

I returned just in time for Spiritual Direction. I brought my dialogs to Sister Debbie to discuss.

I told her that Mother had carried me to the cemetery across the street to cry at my brother's grave. He'd drowned when she was five months pregnant with me.

I wondered if I had trouble separating my sadness from others' sadness. I noted that this gave me great empathy that helped me in Spiritual Direction and in my work as a psychiatrist. She noted that my inner Susan seemed to be very attuned, and compassionate, about what others were feeling, like Xavier. Debbie encouraged me to continue my dialogs and to be open to the wisdom of my inner Susan.

Next on the agenda was the School's private Eucharist. One of our classmates, Father Bruce, celebrated.

Afterwards BA and I made a slow circuit of the grounds, returning just in time for Vespers. Then we headed for the base of the stairs to the dining room where we waited for the bell. A rolling heated cart had been placed where the cafeteria tables had been for breakfast and lunch.

Dinner was turkey Salisbury steak with buttered noodles and broccoli. It wasn't bad.

Afterwards I went downstairs to the break room and called Sarah. We prayed over the phone for her back. I retired to my room to listen to Sarah's tape, mount the new pictures on the wall and read until bedtime. I finished *Beyond the Mirror* and turned out the light.

taking a few minutes
to lie in bed
and enjoy bugsong

EIGHT

1995, Pecos Benedictine Monastery, Week II, Sunday

Michael and I hiked the mountain at six, still breathless on the uphill but sharing our stories on the downhill. We got back in time for chapel.

After Mass the four of us went to our rooms briefly and then met at Coy's car for our trip to Harry's.

We chatted companionably on the trip. Soon the crunch of gravel under the tires signaled that we had arrived at Harry's.

We sat outside at a table in partial sun. Hummingbirds sipped nectar from the flowers all around us. Today I had Chicken Enchiladas with Sour Cream and Green Chile sauce. Divine. Mindful of our trip to Renate's later that morning we skipped dessert.

Santa Fe was just a hop down the Las Vegas Highway. We parked at the Inn at Loreto and began to browse the Indian wares set on tables outside the Chapel at Loreto. We came to a table filled with silver jewelry. The designs were almost lyrical. I found a silver bracelet for Sarah. The sun was in my eyes when I was paying; the silversmith's daughter lifted her umbrella to shade my face.

Five years later there was a small Indian market in Dallas, and my family attended. I recognized the artist's work immediately. I lifted my eyes and met the silversmith's eyes. "Did your daughter enjoy the bracelet that you bought from me in Santa Fe?" he asked, stunning me. Sarah held up her wrist, grinning. She was wearing the bracelet.

BA and I split off from Coy and Michael. We wandered around the square browsing the tables and sidewalk blankets filled with jewelry and pottery. I bought four turquoise napkins and a cookbook written by one of Georgia O'Keefe's assistants. Later, the four of us met and walked a block to the Museum of Native American Fine Arts.

I soaked in information about Native American culture in the area. I am a collector of Pueblo Indian storytellers and pots, so I especially enjoyed the exhibits of pottery. I am also a potter. The pottery from Acoma Pueblo has always been my favorite. I love the white clay, the thin walls of the pieces and the amazing, virtuous detail of the decorations on the pieces.

That day I learned that all symbols on Native American pottery are prayers, either prayers for the hunt or prayers for rain. It is impossible to farm east of the Continental Divide, where all the pueblos are, without praying daily for rain.

The next year I would take my Pueblo pottery to Sarah's school and teach her class about how the Indians would pray before they set out to gather the clay; pray as they refined the clay; pray as they remixed it with water; pray as the pots or storytellers were constructed; pray as they were glazed and as they were fired. It turns out that you can talk about prayer in the schools if it is culturally relevant!

After our visit to the museum, we headed back towards Pecos, stopping at Renate's Good Food. We parked in her gravel lot and headed for a small white building with lace curtains in the windows. A pot of cascading blue Abelias hung over the door stoop. Inside was a small dining room with a trio of curtained windows on each wall. We took a table and Renate came over with menus. Her tiny frame and accent identified her as Eastern European. Both BA and I chose sausages and potato salad.

The cold potato salad was divine. The potatoes had been sliced into paper thin layers and dressed with a wonderful dressing. BA sweet-talked Renate into revealing that the dressing was homemade sour cream and homemade mayonnaise with salt and pepper.

For dessert we all ordered Renate's apple strudel with her homemade vanilla bean ice cream. No words were spoken as we devoured it. Just tiny Mmmms from the backs of our throats.

We headed back to the monastery. I retired to my room for a nap.

Afterwards I visited the snack room for some tea. There I met two world-class-talky strangers. I escaped as soon as I could. Interacting with them upset me deeply, in a very familiar way. I began a right-hand/ left-hand dialog. Again I chose purple and green.

Me: How did you feel when we talked to those two people?

Little me: They talked too much! Like Mother!

Me: They talked too much, like my mother?

Little me: Yes.

Me: How did you feel when Mom talked too much?

Little me: Squeezed. No breath.

Me: You felt as if the breath was pressed out of you?

Little me: Want to talk half. Me not there for them.

Me: You wanted to talk half of the time. You felt like your presence was not really acknowledged as a person?

Little me: Yes.

Me: And that made you feel squeezed?

Little me: Yes.

Me: Father Michael squeezed you.

Little me: Yes.

Me: What he did was an abandonment.

Little me: Yes.

Me: Your dad squeezed you and you couldn't breathe.

Little me: Yes.

Me: Ethel talked and you weren't there either.

Little me: Yes.

Me: So maybe it is all crashing together, the abandonments of Father Michael, Dad and Mom.

Little me: Yes.

Me: Squeezed, no breath, not there. That's a lonely feeling!

Little me: Yes.

Me: Did you feel like you were bad when they did these things?

Little me: Not bad, not there.

Me: You didn't feel like a bad person?

Little me: NO!

Me: What feelings did you have?

Little me: ANGRY!

Me: You felt angry that they hurt you and abandoned you at the same time?

Little me: YES!

Me: That is awful. I will try to be there for you always.

Little me: OK. Don't get too busy and forget me!

Me: I'll do my best.

I read over the dialog. Once again I was stunned by the wisdom and clarity of this younger part of myself. And once again I was filled with bubbling joy.

Soon it was time for Evening Praise (Vespers). I invited my younger self along. We stopped to look out the window at some magenta cosmos growing outside the screen. Because I was already bubbling, Evening Praise lifted me into the stratosphere.

Dinner was turkey Salisbury steak. Yum yum. Not. The four of us ate lightly and walked together until Compline.

Afterwards, I called my Sarah and told her about the bracelet. She seemed excited. We prayed for her back. She was enjoying the cards she was opening every day. I told her that I was enjoying her tapes and photos.

I skipped the video that night and retired to my room. I rewound the tape from Sarah and played it from the beginning. I mounted the two new photos on the wall. I reread my journal from the beginning, including the dialogs. Then I picked up *Love is the Link* and read for a few minutes until huge yawns enticed me to turn out the light.

racing towards me
a stripe of sunlight
bearing a butterfly

NINE

1995, Pecos Benedictine Monastery, Week II, Monday

The walk up the mountain was exhilarating. I was less breathless every day.

Mass was the usual: wonderful Praise.

Breakfast was a joy sitting with my good friends.

Both classes that morning were taught by my thought-buddy, Father Paul. The topic was the Myers-Briggs Personality Typology. Myers and Briggs were a pair of Jungian psychiatrists, a mother and daughter. Paul explained that the typology was based on preferences between four things:

Introversion v. Extroversion (*Wanting to spend time alone v. Wanting to be with people)*

Intuition v. Sensing (*Using your intuition v. Using your senses*)

Feeling v. Thinking (*Using your feelings v. Using your thoughts*)

Judging v. Perceiving (*Being planful v. Being spontaneous*)

Each time I had taken the test before I'd come out INFJ, just like Meyers, Briggs, and every other psychiatrist on the planet. INFJ means that I was *Introverted/ Intuitive/Feeling and Planful).* When Paul handed out the scorings from Friday, I was very surprised to find that I came out ISTJ, a switchover in the two middle areas of Intuition/Sensing and Feeling/Thinking.

INFJ (old) meant I was *Introverted/ Intuition focused /Feeling oriented and Planful.*

ISTJ (new) meant I was *Introverted/Sense oriented/ Thinking oriented and Planful.*

At first I was very surprised, but as I thought about it, I remembered the rebelliousness I had felt each time I had taken the test. For each test item I'd had to choose between two things. I never wanted to choose between them. Each had seemed desirable. I had reluctantly chosen one of each pair, all the while wanting to choose both. I was glad that I had Spiritual Direction that afternoon. I was hoping that Sister Debbie could sort this out for me.

We went up to lunch. Oriental turkey salad again. Tasty.

After lunch, when the others went off to Physical Wellness, I went back to my room and did a dialog.

Me: Good Afternoon, Susan of God, welcome to Monday.

Little me: Uck.

Me: Uck? You are not happy?

Little me: No.

Me: What are you feeling?

Little me: Heart racing. Overwhelmed.

Me: Your heart is racing? You feel overwhelmed?

Little me: Yes.

Me: Pressure on chest.

Little me: Hard to breathe. Too many people. Too much to do.

Me: You feel like someone is pushing on your chest. It is hard to breathe. There is too much to do. Too many people here.

Little me: Yes. Can't do everything. Letters from home. Write back. Exercise. Juggle. Call Sarah. Quilt. Too many people to talk to.

Me: You feel pressure from outside to do everything, to answer letters from friends at home, to exercise alone, to work on juggling, to keep in touch with Sarah and her dad, to quilt and that there are too many people here.

Little me: Yes.

Me: Is there pressure from inside about these things?

Little me: Yes. Be nice. Smile. Don't cry. Do it all.

Me: What would help?

Little me: Another Sabbath. Like Sundays at home.

Me: How do you feel now?

Little me: Out of control.

Me: You feel out of control?

Little me: Yes.

Me: You are out of control. You always will be, just like everyone else. There are only 24 hours in a day. People are wildcards.

Little me: Yes. Will-cards. (Note: Little me is making a joke about willfulness.)

Me: Funny! Would you like to go for a walk with the juggle balls?

Little me: Yes.

Me: We can't fix this feeling today. But we can take it easier. Stay alone a little more. We'll have time after Spiritual Direction for being alone again.

Little me: OK. Walk. Juggle.

Me: Let's go.

I put on my sneakers, grabbed the juggle balls and went out the far side door on my hallway. I turned left and passed the orchards and beehives. When I came to the trail to the falls, I turned right and walked until I was abreast of them. I sat on a log and listened to the rush of the water.

Soon my watch told me that it was time for Spiritual Direction. I hurried back, left the juggle balls on my dresser and slipped on my Birks.

I told Debbie about the change in my Myers-Briggs scores. She was unconcerned. She felt that the shift showed growth and a greater acceptance of all sides of things. She told me the more I moved toward the center of an axis, the better I would be at my work. My scores indicated I was in the middle on Intuition/Sensing and Feeling/Thinking, but I was a still a profound Introvert and a profound Planner. She did not think that these two would ever change.

I was very glad to hear this explanation. I had never felt "against" any of the choices on the Myers-Briggs; I had always liked both choices. It was only the requirement to choose one that shaded me toward NF and now had revealed a fondness for S and T.

I returned to my room and pondered this. Soon the bell rang for Vespers and then for supper.

Turkey spaghetti again.

After dinner I called Sarah. We chatted. She was jealous of my going to Harry's. I promised to take her there one day. We prayed together for her back. The other three amigos waited in the classroom while I called her. Then we walked together, making a circuit of the grounds.

The evening class failed to engage me. I gathered my notebook and slipped out. I tended to leave my quilt squares on the chair overnight and tonight was no exception.

I listened to Sarah's tape and posted her photos. I read more in *Recovery of the Inner Child* until I felt sleepy. I turned out the light and fell into a deep sleep.

red hills
peppered with juniper
Georgia on my mind

TEN

1995, Pecos Benedictine Monastery, Week II, Tuesday

The weather for our walk was almost balmy at 60 degrees. We walked surefooted up the mountain with little breathlessness.

On the way back, Michael told the story of making his final vows as a Benedictine. Michael lay face down on the cold stone floor of the chapel, arms out to the side, his body in a cross shape. He could hear the sandaled approach of two monks from the rear, and the soft murmur of silk. He felt the silk burial cloth slide over his feet and legs and up his body until his whole body was covered by the black brocade. He lay there on the cold stones in total darkness, meditating on dying to self and being raised again belonging only to God and to his Community.

How often do I fail to die to self?

The story gave me chills, even though the morning was warm. Truth is, that story still gives me chills whenever I think of it.

Mass was filled with joyful Praise. The Gospel was Jesus' teaching about forgiving seven times seventy. The Abbot invited School members to the microphone to give the homily if any of us felt led. My palms were sweating profusely.

OK, I'll do it.

I stepped to the mike and told a story of forgiveness that had healed a whole family. I had been asked by another psychiatrist to do a consultation on a hospitalized man who was practicing two addictions. The combination can be life threatening. I knew from the treating doctor that the patient was Jewish and that his family had lost 14 members in the Holocaust.

When I went to his room to get him for the consultation I saw his Torah on his nightstand. The gold leaf had been rubbed from the center edges of the pages from his active thumbing of the Hebrew Scriptures.

When we got to the consultation room I surprised myself by diving in with both feet.

"You need to forgive Adolf Hitler," I said in a calm voice.

"God has not forgiven Hitler!" he retorted.

"He has. Why wouldn't God forgive him?"

"He committed genocide" said the man, exasperated with me.

"The Jews committed genocide."

He began to sputter.

"Go and get your Torah. Let's read Joshua, Deuteronomy and Numbers."

He didn't need to get his Torah; he began to tick off the tribes that Israel had slain: Ammonites, Amalekites, Canaanites and other tribes.

His shoulders slumped.

"You have genocide inside of you because of what your people did in slaying those tribes. This is why you are attacking your own body. He blinked, paused and nodded. Jews are spiritual geniuses. Scripture says it in Hosea 9:10 'When I found Israel it was like finding grapes growing in the desert.' You are meant to be a spiritual leader in the recovery community here. Forgive yourself. Forgive Hitler."

He straightened up and looked me in the eye. "I will."

His family therapist called me a week later. The patient had confronted his parents in family therapy, "You need to forgive Hitler."

"You have been reading the New Testament!!" they replied.

"No, I read it in my Torah that you gave me for my Bar Mitzvah."

The man was free. He went on to become a leader in the recovery community on the psychiatric unit.

Everyone in the chapel was watching me raptly.

As I made my way back to the pew where Michael and BA waited, Costanzo grabbed my sleeve to ask me to repeat the Hosea citation for him.

At breakfast many classmates and monastics congratulated me on my sermon.

After breakfast, we came downstairs to the classroom, where Sister Miriam was waiting. She was and is a spry older woman who has held on to every bit of her Boston accent.

Miriam spoke of symbols for healing. The symbols, oil, candles, altars, and the communion cup functioned as road signs on our way to earthly healing as well as signs on our way to the final, ultimate healing. She said that these symbols marked liminal space, a threshold to a new reality.

Lunch was more turkey. Turkey. Turkey. Turkey.

Small Group was outside today. We met at the river door of the J-shaped guesthouse and carried lightweight plastic chairs to the side of the laughing brook under the cottonwoods.

As I did anytime the sun was up very much, I wore an old sailor hat brim down and a loose woven, white cotton shirt over my tee shirt.

During Small Group we spoke of our assigned topic: "Why Do We Offer Spiritual Direction?" We came up with quite a few ideas.

The Holy Spirit is the real Spiritual Director. We just sit in the other chair and help to guide the directee into a primary relationship with the Holy Spirit, a dialogical relationship with the Holy Spirit.

Spiritual Direction cultivates healing and forgiveness and heals fissures in the directee's soul caused by past neglect and abandonment.

Spiritual Direction allows for the gradual spiritualization of life, which allows the directee to attain full psychological maturity. This maturity allows the directee to attain the wholeness that God wants for her.

Every story is a sacred story; the Director bears witness to the directee's story and her suffering and stands with her in the face of life's challenges.

Spiritual Direction and Therapy are both "perfect relationships" in which the Director or Therapist "dies to self" and is present for the sole purpose of serving the other.

There were nods and grins all around as we articulated what we knew.

After group, the men carried the chairs back to the porch. Ann and I set off on a walk. We talked about our girls and how much we were missing them.

Soon it was time for Vespers and dinner.

Turkey meatballs. Not half bad.

I called Sarah and we visited about our days and prayed together for healing of her back.

The evening lecture was by Sister Theresa, "Befriending the Inner Child." This was just what I was trying to do with my right-hand/left-hand dialogs. I was beginning to "get" that my inner child was both in need of compassionate care and a tremendous source of wisdom.

It's like that amazing wisdom that you often see in the eyes of new babies. Wordsworth said it this way, "but trailing clouds of glory do we come from God who is our home." Maybe dialog with my inner child can keep me in touch with wisdom and with God who is my home.

After class I returned to my room and listened to Sarah's tape for the day. Only one photo today. I attached it to the wall.

I lay on my bed for a few minutes looking at the ceiling. I used to do this in med school when I got overwhelmed. The ceiling in my room at Pecos was knotty pine with support beams spaced 18 inches apart. I got up and peered out my window to see if they extended into the hallway. They did.

Returning to my bed, I picked up *Recovery of Your Inner Child* and read for an hour before turning off the light and falling into a dreamless sleep.

lighting candles
little finger crooked
the prioress

ELEVEN

1995, Pecos Benedictine Monastery, Week II, Wednesday

The summer solstice brought another crisp cool morning. We were getting conditioned to the climb and breathed easily on the uphill. We mostly kept silence on the uphill, actually praying instead of pretending. On the downhill Michael continued to fascinate me with stories of life at a nearby Benedictine Monastery. I told stories about the practice of medicine and psychiatry.

Wednesday's Eucharist was uplifting.

Breakfast was the usual wonderful smorgasbord. Ann sat with us again. I taught her to make a nunsuch banana.

Today all three of our lectures were to be about healing and a healing service was planned for the evening. I looked forward to all.

I believe in healing. I believe that the physical laws of nature and the spiritual laws of nature have the same Author and I believe that when both types of law are invoked together miracles happen. I had seen hundreds of miracles by the time I got to Pecos and have seen hundreds more since.

Agnes Sanford in *The Healing Light* said "unlimited miracles are possible." I believe this. When I wrote a monthly column for my church newsletter the header was *DISCOVER THE MIRACLE* and the footer was *BE REALISTIC: EXPECT A MIRACLE*.

The morning class was on "Healing Parental Relationships." The second morning class was "Healing the Inner Child."

That afternoon while my classmates had Physical Wellness I walked around the grounds with two of my juggle balls. I returned to my room and read a few chapters of *The Healing Light*. I have read the book a total of ten times to date, and expect to read it again and again. It is new each time. Mother loved that book. She was part of the Catholic Charismatic Renewal. I have Mother's copy of Agnes' second book, *Sealed Orders*.

I loved the potential for solitude built into our days at the monastery. There were breaks built into every part of the day and long periods of unstructured time for reading, journaling, walks alone, naps, or looking at the ceiling. We were always "done" by 9 p.m.

The healing service that night offered prayer for healing and an opportunity to be "slain in the Spirit." I wanted to try that again. My first experience of this was unsettling and not conducive to trust.

I had been at a retreat for Spiritual Directors and Therapists. The retreat leaders were determined to slay all 150 of us in the Spirit. The two leaders had their hands on me and rocked me. I went down, convinced that they had manipulated my spinal reflexes. As I lay there, furious, I hear a rustling. Jesus came and sat down beside me. He looked in my eyes and took my hand in his warm hands. He raised his head and watched the leaders for a few moments quietly then looked back at me. "Sometimes you Christians do really weird things," He said. I started laughing and couldn't stop. Jesus laughed, too.

Now at Pecos, in a more trusting frame of mind, I went up for slaying in the Spirit. Father Paul prayed over me. He did not touch me. At some point I collapsed. The strong arms of two monks caught me and laid me gently on the floor of the chapel. I lay there in great peace, the peace that passes understanding. I felt safe and I felt that the experience had been true.

When I was ready I got up and took "my" chair by the Guadalupe mural. I noticed that there was a woman sitting near me, a stranger, sobbing her heart out. I pulled out one of the boxes of Kleenex and gave it to her, then moved into the seat beside her and wrapped my arms around her, holding her as she cried.

Later, I went to my room and quickly fell asleep.

dawn
golden poppies
tightly furled

TWELVE

1995, Pecos Benedictine Monastery, Week II, Thursday

Thursday dawned partly cloudy and a little colder. I was glad for my jacket. Michael and I made our way up the jeep trail with confidence. Our cheeks were pinker than usual when we paused to catch our breath at the moaning pine. The wind was up and the pine was moaning.

During the Eucharist, the Abbot asked if any of us wanted to give the sermon. My palms were sweaty. I sighed and made my way to the microphone and tapped it with my finger. Nothing. Brother Ed tried his best to get it to work. To no avail.

Raising my voice as best I could (Until recently I have been a volume impaired person) I told the story of a friend in the prayer ministry who was in an area of law enforcement devoted to crimes against children. He called me one day and asked me to meet him at the church for prayer. When I got there he was with his prayer partner, a church worker; her dad had been in law enforcement and she had a special heart for "cops."

Our friend told us of his struggle. A little girl had been kidnapped; hope was fast evaporating that the child would be returned alive. Our friend was filled with rage. He asked us to pray that God would grant him the grace to forgive the offender.

We laid hands on him and prayed. At the close of our prayer, our friend was bathed in joy. He burst into tears and sobbed for several minutes, soaking his huge cotton handkerchief. He hugged us and left.

Thirty minutes later he called us. Fifteen minutes after we had prayed for our friend, the perpetrator had walked into a police station, handed over the child, and turned himself in. I finished the story and started back to my seat. I was weeping and noticed that many others in the chapel were weeping also.

As I walked back to my seat, the Abbot stood and asked Sister Geralyn to lead us in a verse of "Amazing Grace." The congregation stood and sang. Even more burst into tears.

After Eucharist, it was off to breakfast. Then most of my classmates piled into vans for a trip to Chimayó, New Mexico, a site associated with healing. A tiny chapel there had a hole in the floor of a back room and the hole gave forth an inexhaustible supply of red earth. The earth was reputed to bring physical and spiritual healing. The group would then go on to sample New Mexico cooking at a restaurant nearby.

I had decided to stay at the monastery and read, walk and reflect. After giving my louder-than-my-usual-voice homily I had felt persistently unsettled, so I returned to my room for a right hand, left hand dialog. This time I used green and hot pink. Here's the dialog:

Me: Wow. When we spoke up so everyone could hear us it was awful. I felt so vulnerable, so unable to defend myself, so upset, so afraid. I think my spirit left my body. I couldn't calm down, my heart raced. I was uncomfortable for at least 45 minutes. I couldn't enjoy the worship, I felt impatient with the one using the ladies room. I wanted to run to my room. My patience, my ability to be present to the moment, my relaxation, and my compassion were all lost. I feel better when I put my hand on my chest. Do you know why this happened?

Little me: Loud voices. Angry. Fight.

Me: My loud voice reminded me of angry, fighting voices like my parents?

Little me: Yes. Hit. Smash.

Me: They hit each other and smashed dishes.

Little me: Yes.

Me: But I wasn't angry, just louder than usual. I was so loud so they could hear me, so that I could share.

Little me: Feels angry!

Me: It would help me so much if I could speak louder. It would help me if I could feel calm when I speak loudly. I could do God's work so much better.

Little me: Yes.

Me: How can we become more comfortable with my happy, teaching, loud voice?

Little me: I like teachers!

Me: Teachers need a happy loud voice.

Little me: I see.

Me: What if I told you it was a happy teacher voice?

Little me: OK…

Me: That did not sound entirely OK.

Little me: I feel quiet.

Me: Are you OK with this new idea?

Little me: I think so. I've been afraid for so long.

Me: Could we try it?

Little me: OK. I'll do my best.

Me: I might use it to call to Sarah. I almost never yell at her. I'll tell you it's my happy teacher voice before I do it.

Little me: OK.

My mind went back to the fights my parents would have after the kids were in bed. We'd hear them yelling and smashing dishes. They broke all of the china and got dark aqua melamine plates that wouldn't break.

Once my dad hit my mom in the head and broke his arm. I remember being in the cafeteria eating donuts after church with my dad. A man asked him how he broke his arm and he said that he'd hit mom in the head, jokey like. The man turned to me and asked if it was true. I said yes. I got in a lot of trouble for telling the truth that day.

I thought about the way people clap along with the beat to some church songs and how I never do.

I remembered growing up in my family. My mom had a fiery temper and would often lash out with a quick smack. Somehow, I had the ability to fly underneath her radar.

My siblings, several of whom had Attention Deficit Disorder, did not have this ability. Mostly Mom would make her list every day and wait for Dad, the family disciplinarian, to get home.

He would have the offender bend over my parent's bed and he would beat them with his belt. All of us were required to stand there and watch.

I can still feel the sting of the belt on my legs but more than that, I remember the sound of that belt hitting my dear siblings. I especially hated it when the redheads were beaten, because the stripes would remain on their legs for almost a day.

I think that clapping with the music in church reminds me too much of the sound of Dad's belt hitting me and the other kids. Unfortunately, this insight has not helped me much; as I write this I still won't clap to the music in church.

Ultimately, my identification with my sibling's beatings helped me to come back to Jesus. In 1987 Sarah's dad wanted to go to the mall where there was a big exhibit about the Shroud of Turin. I watched Sarah, then 5, while her dad viewed the extensive exhibit; there were pools and fountains all around and I wanted to keep her safe.

When he was done I turned Sarah over to him and walked through the exhibit. I didn't feel much at first. Then I saw the panel illustrating the instruments of torture used on Jesus. BAM!!! I was overwhelmed. I wanted to tear my clothing. I felt everything I had ever felt for Him in my life. I stood there, trying to take it all in. He was back for me.

Just as I had identified with the 'stripes' of my siblings, I came back to Jesus by identifying with his stripes. This summer, I wore stripes, too. *By His stripes you are healed.*

In the Eastertide of the next year, I would be overwhelmed at the Good Friday services, truly "getting" that I was attending

Jesus' funeral. I never went to a Good Friday service again after that. For one, I "got it" and for another, I didn't want to feel that sorrow again; I did not feel that it was required of me. I loved Jesus with my whole heart. I had given my life to serving him by serving others. I sought his face in everyone that I met. I had given my life to helping people who were Christian "fall in love" with Jesus Christ. Attending His funeral each year was no longer necessary.

At three o'clock I heard the footfalls and laughter of my class-mates as they returned from their trip to Chimayó. Shortly thereafter I heard a knock on my door. BA was there. We hugged. I saw a smudge of red dirt on her nose and a fine dust of red dirt on her white skirt.

I slipped on my shoes and we set out using the back door near the nuns' dormitory. BA was excited about her trip. She'd brought back a vial of the dirt from the church at Chimayó.

I told her about the red dirt on her nose and she wiped it off with her right thumb. "Hold still a minute," she said. With dignity, authority and quiet intensity BA reached up and made a cross on my forehead with the dirt on her thumb, saying the words from the Baptism Liturgy of the Episcopal Church, "Su-san, you are sealed as Christ's own forever."

BA takes seriously Jesus' charge that we are to be a kingdom of priests!

I told BA of my dialog and my pesky low-volume voice. The insights of that day were helpful to a degree, but my low-volume voice persisted for 16 years until I was well into writing this book.

It was only when I spoke publicly about my abuse that I got my voice back. I had flown to New Orleans to deliver an address to a group of 70 Sexual Abuse Nurse Examiners, appropriately called SANE nurses. As I walked to the podium I learned that the microphone was broken. Expecting my usual low-volume voice to prevail, I asked the nurses in the back to raise their hands whenever my voice dropped and they couldn't hear me. To my surprise, no one raised a hand. I had my voice back!

As I spoke to the nurses that day, 70 pairs of kind eyes were fixed on me, following every word as I read pages from this book. Because they were medical professionals I was able to recount medical details about how the abuse affects my daily life physically, emotionally and spiritually.

I had been silenced for 57 years and now I could speak in a voice loud enough to reach the back of a huge conference room.

Later, at the airport, I realized that I no longer bore the shame of what had happened. I had given the shame back to my abuser, Father Michael, to whom the shame truly belonged.

I had my voice back and I was free.

At the monastery that day BA and I circled the grounds several times. When we heard the bell for Vespers we were a distance away, so we hurried to the chapel without changing shoes. We arrived just in time.

In honor of my classmates being stuffed from their lunch at Chimayó, dinner was light. Turkey meatloaf and green beans, no starches.

After dinner, I called my Sarah and we chatted about our days and prayed together for her back.

I skipped the video that night and read in my room until it was time to listen to Sarah's tape and turn out the light.

late for chapel
rushing past
all the haiku

THIRTEEN

1995, Pecos Benedictine Monastery, Week II, Friday

I awoke to bugsong, heart pounding. I had it in my mind that this was the day that Sister Geralyn would teach us Creative Movement i.e., Dance. I checked the syllabus. Today was Geralyn but the day was devoted to Non-Verbal Revelation through Arts and Journaling. *Whew!!! I don't have to deal with Dance until tomorrow!*

I got ready for the walk up the mountain and met Michael by the grandfather clock. It was a crisp morning and the heavy wooden door creaked as I opened it. As I let the door close I let my fingers slide over the carving of the descending dove.

We quickly made our way to the jeep trail and ascended, each of us praying silently. We reached the moaning pine and immediately turned back, not needing to catch our breath any longer.

We chattered happily on the way "home" then each went to our own room to change shoes. As I entered my room I saw the Abbot slip quietly out of his room four doors down from mine and head toward the chapel. I changed my shoes and followed.

Today was the Feast of the Sacred Heart of Jesus. I found myself thinking of statues that I had seen of the Sacred Heart. In these statues Jesus' heart is huge, almost covering his whole chest. His Heart is also radiant with light in these statues. I found myself thinking of the "heart chakra" of Eastern Medicine, an energy center in front and behind the heart. *I wonder if the statues were "really" about Jesus' huge, open heart chakra.*

Thankfully I did not have sweaty palms that day, so another student gave the sermon.

Breakfast was genial, with Ann joining us again. She and I both made nunsuch bananas.

After breakfast Geralyn led us to the downstairs lounge where she had set up folding cafeteria tables. The tables were laid with

12x18" sheets of plain construction paper and boxes of crayons. We took our places at the tables. I could not help but look out the windows that revealed the Pecos River Valley in all of its glory. *I remember how the nuns in grade school would set up our desks to face the windows in fall and spring, but in winter they'd turn the desks around so we wouldn't see the snow and focus on it instead of our lessons. I am so glad that Geralyn understands non-verbal revelation!* I suspected that Geralyn WANTED us to look out the window and see God's glory revealed.

Geralyn asked us to make a face-sized circle on our paper with our crayons, and then fill it in as we pleased. I took a turquoise crayon and made a nine-inch circle. In the center of the circle, I made a diamond with curved sides six inches across. I filled the rest of the circle with Vs, triangles, crescents and dots, using turquoise, purple and red crayons.

When I was done, I saw that many of my classmates were still working, so I went to the window and drank in the Pecos Valley. To the right was an enormous swampy area with cattails and willows. To the left was the laughing brook lined with the trees that it nourished. I could see the duck pond near the end of the brook and the river beyond that. I was filled with gratitude and wonder.

Soon Geralyn called us back to our seats. She handed us black pens and asked us to write whatever came to our minds when we viewed our mandalas. Here is what I wrote:

*The diamond in the center is the God shaped hole that is in me. It pokes into every corner of my being. The decorations work together to create a welcome place for God to dwell. The God shaped hole is sur-*rounded by blue light, healing. (Note: Many persons in the healing ministry see blue light when they pray for healing). *The dots create a pointillism that portends a sermon, an epiphany.*

Some spaces are filled; some are empty, waiting for God to fill them. These spaces wait trustingly like baby birds wait for their mothers to come with food. The four points of the God-shaped hole create a moral compass. The purple dots are the kind, loving eyes of those who have gone before; those who share the same spiritual gifts as I. They are interceding for me, for my path, for my contribution to the world, for my contribution to the Kingdom.

The crescent moons in the design remind me of the crescent moon that I saw on my first walk up the mountain, on the jeep trail. That day I thought of that crescent moon as the fingernail of God.

I sat back and read what I had written. *Wow!* The "wow" reminded me of how I felt after I did one of those right-hand/ left-hand dialogs. The "stuff" that comes out is amazing.

We had a 15-minute break. Geralyn told us to meet her near the gym after the break.

I went to my room to get my oversized white shirt and my sunhat. Geralyn was sitting in the dirt outside the gym when we arrived. We gathered around her. She read to us from Ezekiel 37: *The Spirit of God took me to a valley where the ground was covered with bones and they were very dry...Prophesy to the bones...Tell them that I am the Sovereign Lord...I am breathing breath into them and bringing them back to life...the bones were covered with flesh and stood up.*

Geralyn picked up a basket filled with 8" pieces of driftwood from the Pecos River. She passed it around and asked each of us to take a piece of dry driftwood. Geralyn asked us to hold the wood in our hands and to meditate on the Scripture.

I held my stick, eyes closed, and ran my fingers over it, memorizing every contour. Then I "saw" it spring to life. The wood became wet and newborn leaves sprang from it. I could "feel" them with my hands. The baby leaves were soft and pliant, the kind of new leaves in which the wind could only make a whisper. I felt great peace.

Geralyn gently invited us to return from our meditation. She asked us to share our experience. One by one my classmates related how these dry, dusty sticks reminded them of their dry spirits. All 31 people went before me. I panicked and sighed and parroted back their experiences of dry sticks instead of my own experience of lush new growth.

I am not sure what I feared. Being different? Surely the gentle souls spending four weeks living in a monastery would not have stoned me. My experience was exactly what the Scripture had said: new life!

At lunch, over turkey Sloppy Joes, I confessed to my amigos and apologized for not being true to myself or to the Scripture. Later I would write to Geralyn and apologize, also.

After lunch I returned to my room and journaled about my shocking failure to share my true experience with the driftwood. I still find it hard to believe that I did that. That night when I spoke with Sarah I shared my experience and advised her never to do what I had done, to always be true to herself. As I was writing this I spoke with her and she still remembers this conversation clearly.

I rested for a while and then it was time for Small Group

We met outside again, sitting in the shade of the trees along the laughing brook. We started with prayer requests. We then turned to our topic for the day "the First Session with a New Directee." Many helpful themes came up.

The Directee has come to find God, not you; sit with them. Give them the gift of time, of presence and of deep listening. They have come to tell their story.

If possible, have some sacred symbols in the room. These symbols connect the Director and directee to the feeling energies of the soul. These symbols bridge the physical and the spiritual reality.

Meet the directee with integrity and with the promise of confidentiality. Be at home with silence; silence can be sacred. Meet them with a quiet intensity.

Recognize the directee's hunger to move beyond her current state.

Be alert to the meaning of the directee's posture and the hidden meaning behind the words they chose.

The discussion was spirited.

I returned to my room to rest up from the effort. I lay down and slept until I heard the Vespers bell. I splashed water on my face and hurried to the chapel. Coy was in his corner at the end of the row; Michael and BA were already in their places.

Dinner would be turkey Salisbury steak, an interesting and tasty concoction, if you didn't know that it was turkey.

I called Sarah. She made turkey noises when I described dinner. She shared her day and we prayed for her back.

Compline was combined with another Prayer Ministry time. I went up and asked that God show me anything I was doing to contribute to my troubled marriage and I asked for healing for my marriage. I received the prayer gratefully although I didn't feel much or gain new insights.

After the service I took my introvert self back to my room and read for a bit before climbing into bed.

early evening
sunflowers already
turned toward dawn

FOURTEEN

1995, Pecos Benedictine Monastery, Week II, Saturday

I awoke in a panic again. *Today* was when Sister Geralyn would teach the Liturgical Dance class. *Ugh!* My heart was a kettle-drum beating in my chest just thinking about it.

There would be no walk up the mountain today. Michael and Costanzo were already in a car hurrying to the Christ in the Desert Monastery near Abiquiú New Mexico, 90 miles away. This is the monastery where Michael had lived for 17 years. I decided to walk around the grounds instead of "going off the grid" alone, up the jeep trail. Saturday mornings the Community had a private Eucharist and the School could sleep in.

I walked alone, making two circuits of the 900 acres. When I heard the bell in the bell tower ring, I meandered back toward the chapel, giving the Community plenty of time to take their places in the chapel. I didn't want anyone in the community to see me slipping into the small consultation room just off the chapel.

I took my place, hands on either side of the mosaic of the bread and cup. I leaned into the wall and began to pray quietly in tongues for the Community. I continued praying until I heard them leave the chapel and until I heard my classmates in the hall outside, making their way to our classroom, to wait for the breakfast bell.

When the dining room gong sounded, we trooped up the stairs. At the landing I ran my fingers lightly over the point of the lodge pole pine at the turn of the stairs and over the black, heavy chain that served as a stair rail for the top half of the stairs.

Coy, BA and I sat together, missing Michael's witty presence. Beaming, BA showed off a card from her granddaughter. It was a huge card of a cutout princess, her dress covered in glitter. BA entertained us with tales of her beloved granddaughters.

We had two classes that morning. They were deeply linked. The first was taught by Abbot Andrew about Biblical archetypes or patterns; the second by Sister Debbie, the psychologist, about Psychological Jungian archetypes (patterns).

Abbot Andrew taught using Abraham as an example of how God works in each of our lives. He spoke of God's calling on Abraham's life; God's promises to Abraham; Abraham's response; the fulfillment of God's promises and, finally, God's testing of Abraham's faith.

I can relate to that! I thought of the calling on my life to forgive, to be a psychiatrist and a Spiritual Director and to see Christ in every person. When will my tests end? Never. I sighed. I realized that new callings on my life would continue to unfold throughout my life.

The Abbot spoke of how Scripture; tradition; our observations of God's work in creation and our impressions of Jesus, the Word made Flesh, can help us in our response to the callings on our lives.

After a 15-minute break, which BA and I spent sitting on the wall near the hollyhocks, we returned for Sister Debbie's lecture.

She spoke of the psychological archetypes laid out by Swiss Psychiatrist, Carl Jung. Debbie said that patterns and archetypes are food for our souls as we muddle our way through life.

"You cannot understand the world if you do not understand paradox," she said at one point. I flipped into reverie.

Wow. Paradox is the story of my life. I LIVE on Planet Paradox: how to juxtapose the good and bad in Father Michael, in my parents, in the surgeon who didn't care if I lived or died. The relationship between forgiveness and paradox. How to embrace paradox.

Still in reverie, I thought about how paradox had consumed me in college. I had been furious about the paradoxes presented to me in physics class and went to great lengths to resolve them in my mind.

In "regular"' physics I learned that you can determine the position and the momentum of an object at the same time. Then when I studied quantum physics, oops, you cannot know the position and momentum of an object at the same time.

This infuriated me. Since I was a child I had depended on science to bring certainty into my life.

To try to reconcile this I took a course that was way over my head, "Partial Differential Equations." I had learned that if position and momentum were both eigenvalues of the same Eigen function (i.e., both solutions to the same equation), you COULD know position and momentum at the same time.

I learned enough in partial differential equations to regain my faith in science. This was immensely important because by then the abuse had stolen my faith in God.

Slowly coming back to regular consciousness I heard Debbie talking about Jung. She touched on the one thing that I really like about Jung, the concept of the Ego Ideal versus the Shadow.

The Ego Ideal is the nice person we think we are. The Shadow is the part of us that holds the parts of ourselves that we do not like to think about: painful parts like when we were shamed; when we were powerless; when we were victimized; and when we were afraid; and when we did bad things.

She went on to describe some of the Jungian Archetypes. She lost me there. I am kindly disposed toward Carl Jung, and respect-ful of his contributions, but I just don't "get" him. I try, but my brain is not wired for his ideas, except for the concepts of Ego Ideal and Shadow, which I find extraordinarily helpful.

A lot of people are crazy about modern Jungian writers, Thomas Moore and Eckhart Tolle. I pick up their books and they may as well be written in Greek. I honor these books, but I cannot "get" them. I bent my head over the quilt square I was working on.

Lunch was turkey spaghetti. Not bad. We talked about the movement class coming up that night. BA was excited about it. Coy and I were not. He had on that straight face that he had when the Abbot sat with us before our jailbreak. I resolved to keep that face plastered on mine during the class that night.

After lunch I grabbed a scissors and went out into the fields to cut grasses for the flower arrangements that I'd agreed to make for our School Eucharist at 3 o'clock.

I had told the Sister Sacristan that I would be creating a Zen meditation on grasses. Her face told me that she was freaking out. I quickly reassured her that Zen Buddhists had no theology at all, just a way of living. She relaxed a bit, dragging her toe back and forth on the tiles.

While cutting great bunches of the native grasses, I found some tiny bright yellow flowers in huge sprays, a bit like "baby's breath" flowers. I came back to the Sacristy where the nun had left me two green glass vases. Two of the grasses were bushy and one had a straight habit. I made the first arrangement and then made the second arrangement the "mirror image" of the first. I placed them on either side of the altar then returned to my room for rest and reading.

The Eucharist was conducted by a priest from our class. Michael and Costanzo were still at the other monastery.

Dinner was turkey Salisbury steak. Michael was back and enthused about visiting his old haunts. He was still glad to have left that monastery but he had many happy memories of his time there.

Glad to be a foursome again, we walked together around the property, staying on the road so that we did not have to change shoes.

When we got back from the walk, I called Sarah. We visited and I prayed for her back. I went back to the room and listened to the tape she had made for that day and put the new pictures on my wall.

At seven we gathered in the classroom; Geralyn again led us to the lounge under the chapel. She had pushed all of the furniture to the outer edge of the room. I took a position facing the windows so that the view of the Pecos River Valley could comfort me while we did the exercise.

I pasted the "sitting with your superior" face on. Geralyn led us through some choreographed movements. It was torture to me. When I was able to get out of my pain, I looked around. Sure enough Michael and Coy were doing the straight-faced thing, too. BA however was really into it. She flowed freely, playfully and joyfully. She even added some of her own moves.

As soon as we were released, I fled to my room. In fact, I was the first one up the steps to the main level. I scrubbed my hands, arms and face to rid myself of the class and sat down to read.

Soon weariness overcame me and I crawled under the covers and fell into an exhausted sleep.

sunlit chapel
the wastebasket
ablaze with red

FIFTEEN

1995, Pecos Benedictine Monastery, Week III Sunday

Sunday dawned cool and clear, with bugsong transitioning to birdsong.

Michael and I hiked up the mountain. He was full of happiness and stories about his visit to Christ in the Desert the day before; he talked all the way to the "top" and back down. The thing that fascinated me the most about his account was that when he entered the monastery as a novice they took away his watch. He would live in obedience to the bells for awakening, for the monastic offices and for meals.

I realized that none of the monks at the monastery wore watches. Michael confirmed that with the exception of the monk responsible for ringing the bell in the bell tower, no monk wears a watch.

When the bell rings, the monk has a few minutes to bring what he was doing to a close and then hurry to the chapel. Michael said that the usual "call" of the bell was five minutes before a monastic office was to begin.

The monastic offices observed at Pecos were Morning Praise/Eucharist (Lauds); Vespers (before dinner) and Compline (before bed).

Other Benedictine monasteries have a more complex schedule. One of the things that Costanzo's visit would cause was the reinstitution of some of the "missing" Offices.

I was fascinated by Michael's story of his watch being taken away. I am driven by the clock, mostly because of the schedule I keep at work, appointments with others, and service times at church. I had 5 clocks in my office and 13 at home!

Before we reached the monastery again that morning, I resolved to take off my watch for the remainder of the School and live by the bells.

The one exception, obviously, would be my 5:30 a.m. alarm, which sounded 30 minutes before the monk's awakening bell. I would also have to refer to clocks for appointments with School members, Small Group and Spiritual Direction. My alarm clock and the grandfather clock would prove sufficient for the duration. Since Coy did the driving on the adventures the four of us took, I would piggyback on his watch on adventures that took us out of earshot of the bells.

We returned to the monastery and parted to return to our rooms to change shoes. I sat on my bed and quietly waited for the bell to summon us to Praise and Eucharist.

The Praise, led by sweet Sister Geralyn, was truly uplifting. Eucharist lifted us further.

When the service ended, the four of us, plus our friend Ann, headed straight for Coy's car for our trip to Harry's. Ann joined BA and me in the back seat. We women talked quietly together in the backseat. The men talked to one another without entering our conversation.

By the time we had driven the 25 miles to Harry's the temperature was a comfortable, sunny 70 degrees. We sat in the middle of the courtyard, surrounded by flowering plants. Hummingbirds and butterflies visiting these flowers delighted us, alighting only a few feet from where we sat.

I ordered a beef and bean tostada with extra cheese. Had to have some cholesterol! By the time we finished breakfast it was almost ten and the day's desserts had arrived. I ordered a slice of carrot cake from Heaven: it was loaded with walnuts, pineapple bits, coconut and carrot shreds. The frosting was a cream cheese one, flavored with almond. I can still taste it today!

We'd all dressed in our hiking boots and long pants so that we could safely visit the grounds of the tiny church again; we were rattlesnake proof. We arrived just as the last few cars pulled away from the early service. We were able to park under the same shade tree as before.

I wandered through the graveyard. The headstones amazed me. It seemed to me that each headstone was constructed with one bag of Portland cement. I could sense that each headstone maker had cut a cross-shaped hole in the earth at his home; the earth in this region can be used to make adobe bricks, so it is very solid and can be worked in this way. The cement had been poured into the dug-out cross. Some had inlaid local stones into the cement; local red-purple rocks or river stones.

A few of the headstones had a photo of the deceased, encased in glass, pressed into the area where the arms of the cross intersected. Each cross had a slightly different shape. Looking at them I felt like my breath was going straight into my heart and swelling it. I was touched by the love poured into each headstone and by the extraordinary creativity of each artist.

My mind wandered to the church graveyard where my earliest ancestors in the U.S. are buried, just outside the church that they built with their own hands in 1770. How comforting it is to me to be able to visit their graves, to connect to them. To connect to the faith they showed in beginning construction on a large church just as the Revolution loomed.

I remembered visiting that church, in Hagerstown, Maryland, during a family reunion. I was looking around the narthex, just outside the sanctuary, and spied a curved glass case. I began to look at the artifacts in the case. I had to kneel to see the lowest shelf. I was so glad that I was kneeling, because I saw my great-great-great-great-great-grandfather's psalm book. In German. The card beside it said that he'd been the Captain of the Regiment from Hagerstown that had fought with General Washington at Valley Forge. He had, it said, read to his men from the psalms every night before bed.

I was glad that I was already kneeling down, because I would have fallen to my knees if his psalm book had been on a higher shelf.

I felt like the paleontologist in Jurassic Park when he first saw the living dinosaurs: he fell to his knees. I knew the paleontologist was thinking: "I've been studying dry bones all my life but it is all true. What I've bet the family farm on is TRUE."

I felt that same way, linked to all of the people in Mother's family who had believed, who had bet the family farm on our faith. Maybe, I thought, that's why I was able to see the "dry bones/sticks" spring to life in Geralyn's class.

My thoughts drifted back to the graveyard where I stood in New Mexico. I sensed that the people there were very glad to have this place and these lovingly made headstones, where they could "visit" their dead and remember their loved one's faith journeys and how those faith journeys continued to affect the living today.

The five of us were very quiet driving back to the monastery, each of us processing the visit to the little church and its graveyard. We decided to skip Renate's in favor of a light lunch at the monastery. We left open the possibility that we might visit Renate's for dinner that night.

I went to my room and napped until the lunch bell woke me. I splashed water on my face, slipped on my Birks and headed for the classroom where I joined my classmates in waiting for the dining room gong to sound. Soon enough we heard it and trooped upstairs.

The four of us sat together and ate our turkey meatballs and salad. The guys had ladled their meatballs onto hot-dog buns, but BA and I ate them "straight." I was still stuffed from Harry's, so I only took two. Faced with another turkey meal at dinner, the four of us decided to go to Renate's for dinner. We would meet at Coy's car after Vespers.

BA and I went for a leisurely walk around the grounds, stopping to feed the ducklings graham crackers. We shared stories of the Healing Ministry and of the miracles we'd seen.

When we rounded the last curve in the path, we saw Coy and Michael waiting for us in the parking lot of the guesthouse. "Let's punt Vespers and go to the Pecos National Monument, then go to Renate's," said Michael the mischievous monk, smiling.

"Cool," I replied, turning to BA to get her assent. She was game. She and I returned to our rooms for our rattlesnake shoes and joined them in Coy's car, which he had chilled while he and Michael waited for us.

The Pecos National Monument was a ten-minute ride from the monastery. We stopped at the entrance to pick up brochures.

The site, on the Pecos River, was rich with history. It was the site of the Pecos Pueblo, a group who traded with the Indians of the Buffalo Plains as well as with Indians from the Rio Grande Valley, far down the Pecos River.

A Spanish Mission had been built on the site; it was now in ruins. A white trading post had been there.

The ruts of the Santa Fe Trail were still visible in the hard earth.

To top it off, the westernmost battle of the Civil War had been fought at Glorieta Pass just ten minutes away from where we stood.

When we visited that day no one else was around. We were able to view where adobe bricks were being made by pulverizing the native soil, mixing it with water, and packing it into brick-shaped molds. The wet bricks were then turned out of the molds to dry in the sun.

Seeing this confirmed the notion formed earlier that day: current residents of this area had dug cross-shaped holes to create molds for their loved ones' headstones, and filled them with concrete.

We hopped on I-25 and drove one exit to Glorieta; Renate's was very close to the exit. Probably the battle mentioned above had been fought, in part, on Renate's land. We crunched into her gravel parking lot.

Entering, I reached up to touch the soft abelias above the door.

I chose potato pancakes with Renate's homemade sour cream and her just cooked, chunky applesauce. BA and I decided to split an order of Renate's potato salad, just for the pleasure of it.

We returned to the monastery stuffed for the second time that day. In spite of the meals out, my khakis were getting loose from all of the hiking and the turkey.

I called Sarah and we chattered about our days. I prayed with her about her back. She said she'd gotten hot all over when I prayed. "That's good!" I replied. "Talk to you tomorrow!"

The bell summoned us to Compline at 7:45 p.m. for a short service.

The syllabus showed a video at 8. I watched it for a while, but it was not deeply meaningful to me, so I returned to my room and wrote down the one thought from the video that had stuck with me. "A mentor helps a person to separate from his/her mother and father."

I listened to Sarah's tape, affixed her photos to the wall and read for a while before climbing into bed.

roadside
a lone white cross
dwarfed by tallgrass

SIXTEEN

1995, Pecos Benedictine Monastery, Week III, Monday

My alarm awakened me at 5:30 a.m. This would be my first full day without a watch. I got ready and consulted the alarm clock. Time to meet Michael.

I slipped quietly down the hall, zigging right then zagging left. I walked past the bell pull, the stairs to the bell tower and the chapel door. I waited by the grandfather clock. It was 5:59 a.m. Michael arrived a minute later. Only six a.m. and I'd consulted a clock twice.

We set out. The moon was a tiny sliver that morning.

Now that we were fitter we could talk the whole time we hiked. I told Michael of my surprise that my "always" Myers-Briggs type had changed. He listened kindly but had no explanation. I told him of the tug that I was feeling to develop my gifts as a writer more.

I told of my first book, *Abiding in Joy*, my pancake book (you know: throw out the first pancake or the first book). I spoke of how I had set aside each morning to write and how much I had enjoyed the discipline of that. I hadn't answered the phone or doorbell. I just put down my head and wrote. I had learned from a much-published author the secret to publishing: "Fingers on Keyboard, Butt in Chair." (FOKBIC)

I said I planned to journal about this dilemma during the afternoon. Michael's only comment was a jokey one that I have never forgotten "Don't wait for the two by four," i.e., if God is calling you to do something, do it without waiting for the 2x4 in the middle of the forehead.

Michael spoke of his desire to end his 40-year career as an altar boy and be priested. He was set to move into the Mother House of his new order in central Texas after the School to begin the process leading to ordination.

We arrived back just in time for the Praise/Eucharist bell. I changed into my Birks and hurried down the hall, following the same zigzag pattern that I'd traced that morning and turned right into the chapel.

I took my place near the Guadalupe mural and stared at the ceiling. I had not noticed it before. The ceiling was two-foot squares painted celestial blue. The squares were divided from one another by intricate white crown molding. Soon BA and Michael joined me. Coy sat at the end of our row, a little apart, as usual.

No sweaty palms, so I was off the hook for the sermon. Another classmate gave it.

Breakfast was jolly. Michael was in rare form, convulsing us with jokes about monastic life.

Our first teacher of the day was the former Abbot, Abbot David. He spoke of the Divine Feminine in each of us. Later, Sister Miriam spoke of the Divine Masculine in each of us. A friend had once told me Miriam would make a good pope. You could see that in her today!

Lunch was turkey Salisbury steak with vegetables and salad. Not bad.

Since I was punting Physical Wellness, I holed up in my room to journal about the strange notion of practicing medicine less and writing for publication more.

I was already writing a long-running column in the magazine *Quilt World: Rx for Quilters*, where I examined health issues particular to women who do needlework.

I wrote a column for my church newsletter about healing: *Discover the Miracle,* where I taught about healing and recounted miracles from the healing ministry at the church.

I also wrote a gardening column for a magazine, *Indoor and Patio Gardening.*

I made columns in my journal, one for Healer, the other for Writer. I had planned to differentiate the skill sets for the two tasks, but it was immediately obvious that there was incredible overlap.

Healing required *listening* to the patient's story. Healing also required *storytelling* when I communicated to other professionals, summarizing the patient's history and leading the other doctor to my questions and conclusions about the situation. Writing required *storytelling* and sometimes *listening*, if I was going to tell someone else's story.

Journaling was something I did in patient charts and for 35 years I had journaled in my personal notebooks.

Communication was a big part of my life. I communicated with patients and with other professionals. For years I'd given talks and workshops to other medical professionals. I'd written a few short articles for scientific journals. In some of my talks I'd brought together science and spirituality. In my quiltmaking column I brought together medicine and needlework.

In my work, I preferred one on one work with patients. I loved the solitude of writing.

I'd always been studious. I knew I could learn the nuts and bolts of writing. I would apply my existing lifelong learning skills.

My former self "clinician" had transitioned to "writer."

I loved to hand write my patient charts. I loved to hand write first drafts of material written for publication.

In my work and in my writing I was a "middlebrow," not an academic. I worked with patients in a private practice setting and I wrote directly for patients.

In both healing and writing I wanted to draw on all that I knew, all that I'd experienced.

I was drawn to the borders between two disciplines. Lifelong learning made me a scientist-physician. I was a physician who looked at the medical-spiritual interface. I was also writing as a physician who looked at the interface of medicine and needlework.

I was very drawn to grow as a writer, and to learn the extrovert parts of writing, publicity and promotion. I was willing to learn to face rejection of my written work. I was willing to learn to work with an editor, to learn the processes involved in publishing.

On the writing side, I had an endless supply of creative juice.

Both my work as a healer and my work as a writer would help people.

I was reluctant to work more at the office. My home life was just too draining.

My therapy patients suffered so much when I had to be away to care for my daughter, who had multiple medical conditions. Writing offered me a very flexible schedule to care for Sarah, her dad and our home. Writing would balance the challenges of my marriage.

I was willing to transition my work life into mentoring younger psychiatrists and into doing more *pro bono* (free) work with high functioning people like clergy and teachers.

I turned to my Myers-Briggs Inventory workbook. My journaling had nailed the changes in me!

In my old type, INFJ, I showed empathy toward the feelings and motivations of others. I wanted meaning and purpose in my work.

These things had not left me. But new abilities had emerged.

In my new type, ISTJ, I was drawn to work with steady energy to complete tasks on time, like writing. I preferred to work alone. I had profound respect for facts, important for a writer.

I glanced at my alarm clock. Time for Spiritual Direction.

Third time today to consult a clock.

I hurried out the river door of the residence hall and walked along the east side of the chapel. A ground squirrel was digging a new burrow. The new earth was darker and wetter than the surrounding soil.

Am I digging a new burrow, too??

Sister Debbie was waiting for me, smiling. *She must have clocks to look at, too!* We sat down and prayed together for a moment, asking God to bless our time together.

I spoke about my journaling and about the shift in my Myers-Briggs. I reiterated how much I hated to have to pick between each pair of choices, that mostly I had liked both parts. She smiled. "People like you tend to be very creative. Probably you are just embracing what was always in you." I relaxed.

I read my journal to her and told her what Michael had said about the two by four. She laughed and reminded me that only I could discern what to do about this shift. She agreed that the shift made sense and encouraged me to pray about it.

After Spiritual Direction, I returned to my room and reread today's journaling. I had to admit that it felt right to begin to write more.

Soon I heard the bell for Vespers. I hurried to chapel for the brief service. The monks left the service through an entrance to the cloister. The rest of us filed out to go down the hall to the dining room to await the dining room gong.

Dinner was turkey spaghetti. Not bad.

After dinner I went downstairs to call Sarah. We laughed together, chatted and prayed about her back.

I returned to my room to read. I listened to Sarah's tape and put the new photos on the wall. My yawns sent me to bed early.

cracks in the shoulder
caulked
by morning glories

SEVENTEEN

1995, Pecos Benedictine Monastery, Week II, Tuesday

My alarm chirped at 5:30 a.m. I lay there hugging my pillow and enjoying bugsong for a few moments, then rose to get ready. At 5:58 I tiptoed down the hall towards the grandfather clock. Michael was already there.

We stepped out into the brisk cool air. I was glad I was wearing my jacket. We hiked quietly for a few minutes.

I glanced at the sky and saw that the moon was now invisible, its dark side facing us: a new moon.

A new moon seems like the perfect day to make a decision. I knew that I was to spend a lot more time writing and that I was to concentrate on working with high-functioning pro bono patients: preachers, teachers and doctors. I surrendered.

I turned to Michael and told him of my surrender. He smiled, "Always let Him have his way! I am glad that you did not wait for the two by four to the middle of your forehead."

Michael spoke of his calling, 20 years back, to be Benedictine. I was surprised to learn that he had to take a vow of stability for the first year. He had vowed to stay on the grounds of his monastery without leaving for 12 months.

"Was that hard for you?"

"Not really. I was pretty committed. I'd visited Christ in the Desert and I knew the drill. Besides, there was so much to learn that year I hardly had time to sleep, much less leave the place."

I wonder if it is harder for the Pecos monks, with the road going past and all of the workshops and retreats.

I thought of the barber chair I'd seen in the laundry room. The monks cut each other's hair! Then they don't have to leave. I thought of the phrase from the Rule of St. Benedict that the monks would form "a tightly bonded community." Cutting one another's hair would certainly lead to that!

We reached the moaning pine and paused for a few minutes. I pointed out the fact of the invisible new moon. We headed back, arriving well before the bell for chapel.

The Praise was unusually uplifting. *Maybe with my surrender to God's will I can have a deeper experience of worship.*

Breakfast was wonderful. It was good to be able to select the day's breakfast from such a plethora of choices. I had a nunsuch banana with my cereal.

Our first class was very interesting, "Healing and the Laying on of Hands." Abbot Andrew and Sister Ann, a registered nurse, taught the class together.

They began by teaching about a healing technique called Noncontact Therapeutic Touch. This technique is both ancient and modern. At that time 56 nurses had earned PhDs studying Therapeutic "Touch."

TT is based on the assumption that human beings are complex fields of energy and that manipulation of these fields by placing the hands near the patient can promote and speed up natural healing.

Why, that is just what prayer for healing does!

The practitioner centers herself then places her hands near the patient, 2-4 inches away, and "reads" the patient's energy field. Some areas may feel hot and some may feel cold. The practitioner then manipulates the abnormal energy field to restore balance. Ann taught us a technique called "unruffling" where you sweep your hands just above a hot or cold area and brush away the abnormal energy.

The Abbot and Ann then compared this technique to praying for someone with the laying on of hands. In Healing Prayer you first center yourself in Jesus, and then assess what the problem is by two means.

The person in need will tell you what they want God to do for them. This gives us a basis for our prayer.

We also ask God to show us how to pray. If there is unforgiveness or anger in the picture, we "unruffle" it by inviting the patient to release the unforgiveness or anger, or we pray for God to give him the grace to do this.

Healing prayer involves a transfer of energy, just like Therapeutic Touch.

That is for sure! When I pray great waves of heat come out of me and can be felt as much as five feet away. Some of my friends see columns of pulsing blue light when we pray. Sarah feels hot when we pray on the phone at night. For sure energy is being transferred.

Ann used the terms "God's energy," "angelic energy" and "human energy." She quoted Matthew 4:11 where angels ministered to Jesus after his temptation in the desert. And she quoted Luke 22:43 where angels ministered to Jesus in the Garden of Gethsemane.

The Abbot and she opined that in both Therapeutic Touch and the Laying on of Hands in Prayer for Healing, God's energy and angelic energy are the agents of change.

They stressed that human energy enters in only in creating the intention to be an agent of healing, the intention to do good.

Lunch was turkey salad on hot-dog buns with a green salad on the side. Not bad.

After lunch I returned to my room to do some journaling. I wanted to have a conversation with my back, which had been aching for two days. I selected purple for my right hand and green for my left.

Me: Hello, back, I want to thank you for all that you do for me. I thank you for holding me up. And helping me stand up and sit and lie down, and for providing support for protection for my vital organs and for helping me carry Sarah.

Little me: I'm glad you noticed me.

Me: You have been signaling me for two days, especially in the morning, that something is wrong.

Little me: Yes.

Me: I don't like the pain. What do you need?

Little me: I'm carrying too much.

Me: You are carrying too much?

Little me: I am.

Me: What would you like to lay down?

Little me: Sarah's dad. He's too heavy.

Me: Carrying him is too much?

Little me: Yes.

Me: I feel the same way. How would you like to lay him down?

Little me: Carry himself. You carry your own self.

Me: You want me to let him carry himself and for me to carry myself.

Little me: Yes.

Me: What does that mean?

Little me: Stop worrying. Pray.

Me: You want me to stop worrying about him and pray for him instead?

Little me: Yes.

Me: I'm not very good at that.

Little me: I know!

Me: Can you tell me how?

Little me: Fix yourself.

Me: What part of me needs fixing today?

Little me: Love him.

Me: You want me to love him, not worry.

Little me: Yes.

Me: "Do" love?

Little me: Call him. Listen like you want him to listen.

Me: OK.

Wow. I didn't see that one coming. I reread the dialog and then went for a walk. My classmates were in Physical Wellness.

First I went and stood under the cottonwood near the gift shop. A breeze was stirring its leaves making a wonderful murmur. I stood there for ten minutes in near ecstasy.

Then I set off along the laughing brook, toward the river. I walked along the dusty dirt road listening to the brook. When I came to the pond I pulled graham crackers out of my pocket to feed the ducklings. They were getting bigger by the day. I sat on a bench and just enjoyed the sunshine and the ripples that the breeze made on the pond.

I am someone who goes to the zoo when it snows; I have the whole zoo to myself. Walking when my classmates were in Physical Wellness gave me the whole 900 acres to myself.

I strolled down to the river and stood on the bridge that led to another mountain. The water was very clear that day. I could see the rocks on the bottom and the small darting fish. The ecstatic feeling that I felt under the cottonwood returned. I stood there enjoying it.

When it faded I took the road along the river and headed toward the waterfall. I stepped into the woods. I stopped to touch the stiff, olive-green horsetails and the bushy needles of the pine with two heads. I came alongside the waterfall and stood there lost in its sound, back in ecstasy.

When the ecstasy faded I headed back, turning left when I got to the circle road. I passed the beehives and the apple orchard. More pinking apples had fallen to the road. I passed the flower gardens outside the nuns' residence. A local woman was watering the flowers. We murmured hellos. She was the only soul I saw on my walk that day.

I returned to my room. It was almost time for Small Group. I walked down the hall and turned right into the short hallway that passed through middle of the building, connecting the two hallways. The short hallway led to the river door.

I glanced at the now-dry dirt outside the ground squirrels' burrow and entered the door leading to the lounge. I walked slowly down the stairs. No one else was about. Physical Wellness must have let out late.

Soon, I heard the laughter of my small group members.

We began with sharing of our experience of the School and prayer requests. Then we turned to our topics for the day, "Facing Decisions" and "Suffering."

We discussed the Jesuit approach to change. This approach teaches that if, as we consider a choice, we experience dread, suffering or negative feelings, we should keep our options open until a solution comes along that allows both heart and mind to embrace it.

One wag added that we should stop what is not working and pay attention to what we are longing for.

We spoke of how to guide a directee using these tenets.

We turned to the issue of suffering. We looked at what Abbot David had said: there is virtue in suffering if a greater good is at stake. Conversely, suffering with no greater good is not to be encouraged.

We discussed the importance of helping our directees to trust righteous anger and to refuse to endure evil.

Afterward, I returned to my room and napped until the bell for Vespers awakened me. I splashed water on my face and stumbled a bit as I followed the hallway to chapel. Michael and BA were already in "our" chairs; Coy took his customary place at the end of the row.

After the short service the monks left en mass toward the Cloister and my classmates and I made our way to the bottom of the stairs to wait for the dining-room gong.

Turkey meatloaf with carrots, cauliflower and broccoli on the side. Ugh. We murmured about going to Harry's on Thursday.

After dinner was a class on "Grief and Loss." No big news for me. I concentrated on my quilt block.

After class I called Sarah. We prayed. She wondered why she got so hot when I was so far away. My nerd daughter and I talked about how some physics phenomena were non-local and speculated that the energy transfer during healing prayer is non-local.

I returned to my room and reread today's "back" dialog. I resolved to do a better job of listening to Sarah's dad when I spoke to him on the weekend.

I picked up my book and read until I felt drowsy. I turned off the light, curled up around my prayer pig and fell into sleep.

psalm verse skipped
coughs
all around the chapel

EIGHTEEN

1995, Pecos Benedictine Monastery, Week III, Wednesday

My eyes opened a few minutes before my alarm chirped. I laid there enjoying the sounds of morning: bugsong slowly giving way to birdsong. At my alarm's chirping, I arose and got ready. I reviewed the syllabus for the day, which was all about forgiveness.

Michael was waiting by the grandfather clock. We stepped out into the cool morning air. Lumpy gray clouds covered the sky. We could smell a hint of rain in the air.

We set out up the mountain. Michael talked about Abbots; the word came from the Aramaic, *Abba*, father. Michael spoke of his vow of "prompt, ungrudging, absolute obedience" to the Superior. He spoke of the "posture of humility" of the monk. Michael certainly had that.

As we paused by the moaning pine, I reflected, *I am not sure I could offer prompt, ungrudging, absolute obedience to any mortal. In fact, I don't do so well with prompt, ungrudging, absolute obedience to God.*

We arrived back before the bell for chapel and went to our separate rooms. The smell of rain was more pronounced by the time we got back. I changed into my Birks as there would be no time to go outside until after lunch.

The Praise songs were wonderful, lifting me up. I felt like I was rising through the heavenly blue of the ceiling into the heavens. The Scriptures were about forgiveness.

Breakfast was quiet but satisfying.

Sister Theresa was waiting for us when we got downstairs. The lights were off again.

She spoke of the need for forgiveness to free us from our prison of anger and resentment. Not every person who hurts us, she said, is capable of appreciating the injury caused by their words or actions.

Mental illness; Mental Retardation; Post Traumatic Stress Disorder; Substance Abuse; being an Adult Child of a Substance Abuser can all impair a person's ability to understand the hurtfulness of their actions.

In many relationships of this nature, the relationship cannot be repaired. We can, she said, come to understand that the person is sick and from that idea, we may ultimately forgive even if we cannot remain in the relationship.

Theresa had on her big beige cardigan again. She began to move around the room, laying her hands on each head and praying at length that the person's "heart of stone" be turned to a "heart of flesh."

When she finished with each person, she reached into her pocket and handed the person two red construction paper hearts. One was folded and had "the gift of forgiveness" written on it.

The other heart had the Scripture verse referred to in her prayer with the cutout of a descending dove on it. This was to remind us that forgiveness is a grace that God gives us, not something that we produce.

Once again, everyone was in tears by the time she finished with the first person. She prayed for each of us, laying her hands on our heads.

She returned to the front after she'd finished and surveyed us to see if we were all OK. She encouraged us to sit quietly until we were ready to go outside for a break.

Our energetic Baptist pastor-classmate was again the first to bolt. The rest of us trickled outside.

The smell of rain was now intense. The skies were very dark. We were a subdued group, many of us still weeping. When it was time for the next session, we filed inside; depositing our soggy Kleenex in the wastebasket Theresa had placed outside the door.

The lights were back on; the old Abbot was waiting for us. Abbot David spoke of forgiveness. He told of his own first Abbot: David was a young monk and had been appointed assistant, secretary and laundryman to the Superior, who was a bit hard to enjoy. David said that forgiving him was an enormous endeavor. He'd spend hours on his knees on the stone floor of the chapel, arms straight out at his sides praying to receive the grace of forgiveness.

I can relate to that. I felt like I had spent half of my time at home praying for the grace to forgive two individuals in my life.

I noted in wonder that I had not been troubled by that unforgiveness since that first healing service. Since then I had felt like I was back up on the ceiling of the operating room, wrapped in love and compassion, not needing to judge anyone.

I hoped that this state was going to last when I went home.

The Abbot said that we would be going into the chapel shortly for Confession, now called the Sacrament of Reconciliation. He said that we were free to speak with one of the priests and to confess our sins and to receive absolution.

He led us to the chapel. The Sister Sacristan had placed dozens of votive candles on ledges, nooks and windowsills all around the room. The candles were a sort of drum roll announcing that something sacred was happening. They twinkled against the dark sky, their light pushing back the darkness. After the Abbot's introduction, eight of the monastery's priests took their places around the edges of the chapel. They wore their white Olivetan Benedictine robes and their purple stoles, further adding to the sacred drum roll. Rolling waves of thunder from the storm outside added to the sacred hush of the chapel.

The Sacrament of Reconciliation is very familiar to me. I celebrate this sacrament every month. I had visited my own Confessor/ Spiritual Director, Mother Delores, a few days before beginning the School, to prepare for the healing and the learning that I hoped would take place during the retreat.

The theme of the previous few days of class had been forgiveness. My many years of prayer and fasting had come to a wonderful culmination during the healing service early in the School, and I had finally been able to forgive my two people.

Now, I wracked my brain to find someone else whom I had neglected to forgive. Prayerfully, I cast my net through my life, searching for someone I needed to forgive. My net came up empty. Then, it was as if Jesus said to me, "Cast your net over here." I cast it and when I pulled it up, I saw myself in the net! My six-year old self, dripping wet. I needed to forgive myself!

My parents had not anticipated the pregnancy with me. I had not felt entirely welcome here.

The very rapid arrival of several siblings had pushed aside my felt sense that it was OK to have needs, or that needs were, in fact, good. I needed to "forgive" myself for being here, and for having wholesome and natural needs.

Of course, God wanted me here, and He, Himself, had given me my needs. My real sin wasn't "unforgiveness," but an inability to accept God's love for me, His gifts to me, including the gift of my human needs, and His plan for me, including my place in my family.

I knew what I had to do, and so I scanned the room to select the priest to whom I would make my confession. I spotted a priest who was just finishing with another penitent. I knew him to be a jovial man, intelligent, orderly, and almost fastidious in his personal grooming.

I sat down at his station, and suddenly I was sobbing. He seemed unconcerned by this and grabbed both of my hands, pinning them firmly with his own. I made my simple confession, and the tears flowed freely. And flowed. And flowed. So did the normal healthy secretions of my nose.

Soon a long strand of clear mucus dangled down from my left nostril. My tears flowed down the strand and dripped onto my pant leg. Occasionally a piece of the mucus would break off under the weight of the tears and melt into the wet patch on my slacks. My hands were still pinned, so I couldn't reach the box of Kleenex laying at our feet.

The rolling thunder continued and once, lightning struck a tree very close to us. Father and I laughed at the sound, our foreheads almost touching. Father began a long prayer for me, asking God to forgive me and to heal me.

My tears continued to flow down the swaying strand of clear mucus. Suddenly, I realized that I was in the midst of a test. To claim my healing, I had to become willing to be seen and hugged with this needy, messy strand of mucus hanging down. Silently, I accepted the test.

I had no sooner accepted "the test," when I remembered Father's penchant for tidiness. I recognized that it was MY test, not his. I couldn't be responsible for his response to my test. I was ready for my test. I was willing to be seen and hugged in my messy neediness. I relaxed and listened to the end of Father's prayer for me.

Apparently, Father had opened his eyes during his long prayer and was aware of the condition of my face. As he ended his prayer, he kept his head bowed, released my hands, grabbed a handful of Kleenex and slid them into my hands. I took them and wiped my face, at peace because I had passed my test. I had confessed my sin and had taken responsibility for changing the patterns that had bound me. I had accepted my existence, my neediness and my occasional messiness. The reaction and response of another was irrelevant. I had heard and accepted God's call to be defined by His love for me.

I returned to "my" seat under the Guadalupe mural and let this sink in. The storm quieted. Soon the old Abbot dismissed us. We trooped back to the classroom to wait for the dining room gong, keeping uncharacteristic silence. Each of us seemed to want to find our own corner to be alone in. I sat in my seat by the windows.

The gong sounded and we trooped upstairs quietly. This was to be a silent meal. We gathered our turkey and sat, focusing mindfully on each bite.

As we walked downstairs, BA asked me if she could walk with me instead of going to Physical Wellness at 2:30. I agreed to pick her up in her room then.

I returned to my room. I taped one of the wet Kleenexes from confession into my journal and closed it, weighting it with books to help it to dry flat.

I lay on the bed, looking at the soft sheen of the knotty pine ceiling, reflecting on my new awareness of my God-given needs. I laughed about Father Fastidious and my mucus.

Fortunately I had set my alarm for 2:25, as I dozed off. I splashed water on my face and put on my sneakers because of the earlier rain. The sun was now out!

I knocked softly on BA's door. She opened it and hugged me tightly. She had on her bright red sneakers and was game to walk the grounds. We circled the grounds several times, dodging puddles, as we talked.

BA's heart was heavy. She wanted to share her sorrow about the "worst" thing she had ever done, which she had confessed in the Service of Reconciliation. I listened, as a Spiritual Companion would, saying nothing. When she was done, I held her in a tight hug for a long time, assuring her of God's love and forgiveness; of God's unfailing love for her; and of my unfailing love for her. She wept. I gave her one of my handkerchiefs. She said that although the person had long ago forgiven her for her act, she planned to call the person and apologize again today.

I shared that many of my more spectacular sins seemed to be buried in shallow graves. Even after a heartfelt confession some sins seemed to need to be revisited from time to time, even though I had accepted forgiveness and absolution when I first confessed them.

Sometimes this repetition made my Confessor squirm since her theology was that I only had to confess these sins once. But now and then I felt that God was calling me to look at them again, to examine the character flaws that had led to the sin, to examine character growth that could prevent the sin from happening again.

I shared with BA that my own confessor of five years was a female Episcopal Priest, Mother Delores. I cherished that she was a woman and a mother. She understood the struggles between my daughter and me because she had gone through the same struggles with her own daughter. She understood the over-the-top passions of the peri-menopause, having experienced them herself.

I shared what had come up today in my pre-confession and confession. BA laughed with me about presenting Father Fastidious with a "mucus challenge." She congratulated me for passing my test and gave me a big hug.

We continued to walk, talking quietly. Once we stopped to look at clouds reflected in a puddle. Suddenly the sun burst through between two clouds. Pinpoints of light reflected up all over our faces and clothing.

On another circuit of the grounds, we saw two goldfinches splashing in a puddle, the water droplets they kicked up trans-illuminated by sun.

We heard the bell for chapel and hurried back to the monastery. Although we had dodged all puddles, my lower pants legs were wet from the grasses in the road. My calves were chilly from the wet. I sat in the first row against the stained glass beside the chapel door hoping to catch the warmth of the sun through the stained glass. During the service I watched a red circle from the piece of round stained glass move up my leg as the sun got lower in the sky.

Dinner was turkey spaghetti sauce over noodles, with green mixed vegetables. In a reverie, I imagined an entire semi truck full of that broccoli/cauliflower/carrot mixture pulling up to the monastery loading dock. I felt like I had eaten a good portion of the truckload so far.

Conversation was subdued all over the room. *I feel subdued, too. It is hard for me to embrace my failings, I feel sad when I do it, but if I am to be whole, I must embrace all that I am, goody- two-shoes and sinner, alike.*

BA and I hugged again at the bottom of the stairs after dinner. She headed into the break room to make her call. I waited in the classroom 'til I saw her come out, giving her privacy.

When she emerged, I called my Sarah. She was excited about helping the teacher make ice cream that day. I promised that she could make ice cream, any flavor she wanted, when she got home from her science camp. We prayed for her back. Again she felt toasty warmth bathe her while I prayed.

I was beat. I returned to my room. There was a note taped to my door from one of our wacky classmates. "There is a light at the end of the tunnel. It's green and it says EXIT." I laughed. I taped it into my journal across from the still damp Kleenex, replaced the weights, fell on the bed and napped until the evening class.

Father Bernie, the Director of the School, taught the evening class. More on forgiveness.

His talk was heavy on Scripture. He discussed the story of the prodigal son and how the older brother was stuck in unforgiveness of his repentant brother. Forgive that you may be forgiven. Pray for those who hurt you. Forgive yourself. Forgiveness is the highest form of love. To want to forgive is to forgive. *Not entirely my experience!*

We went directly from class into the chapel where Bernie led a healing service. I went up and asked for prayer to solidify my forgiveness of myself.

After I took my seat again, I struggled to stay awake. Overwhelmed with tiredness, I slipped out of the chapel early and returned to my room where I took off my khakis and climbed into bed still wearing my tee shirt and socks. I slid into a deep sleep.

rolling thunder
swallows
swirl wildly

NINETEEN

1995, Pecos Benedictine Monastery, Week III, Thursday

I woke before my alarm and lay there, enjoying bugsong. I sat up and turned off the alarm so that it would not chirp, got ready and walked softly zigging right then zagging left, following the long main corridor.

I stopped at the grandfather clock to wait for Michael. A moment later I watched him walk along the main hallway toward me. I had been reading a bit about the "humble posture," which is so important to Benedictines. Michael certainly had this. He kept his energy inside of him; he kept the kind of straight face that any psychiatrist would be proud of and his posture was always deferent. *It is no wonder that the Pecos Community still regards him as a brother monk.*

We set out in silence. We chatted a bit when climbing the mountain, but kept long minutes of silent reflection. We paused at the moaning pine; I looked skyward. There was a sliver of waxing moon visible against the morning sky. *God's thumbnail. He's been leaving his fingerprints all over this world again!*

I never told Michael that I am a survivor of clergy sex abuse. I mentioned having lost my faith for 20 years. That morning, on the way down the mountain, I told him how I had come back to faith, how in med school I had seen the fingerprints of the Creator all over the human body. I watched Michael's humble response, his kindness, his acceptance. *What a wonderful Spiritual Director he must be!*

A clergyman patient of mine had once told me that there were two kinds of Spiritual Directors: "Kick-ass" Spiritual Directors and "Pussycat" Spiritual Directors. I saw in that moment that Michael was a Pussycat Spiritual Director. My own Director, Mother Delores, was a Pussycat Director, sitting quietly and letting me work things out myself. I laughed to myself about my clergyman patient who all but begged me to impose Kick-ass

Spiritual Direction on him. *The trick is to know what each soul needs and to provide precisely what it is needed for each soul.*

We got back well before the bell and went to our own rooms. I changed into my Birks. When the bell sounded, I moved toward the chapel. I nodded to Coy sitting at the end of "our" row and sat under the Guadalupe mural. BA joined me first, then Michael.

It was easy to raise my spirit into Praise in the opening songs.

Brother Matt was lector that day. I watched, smiling inside, as he rolled up his sleeves before reading the Scriptures.

Today was the Feast of Saints Peter and Paul; the Scriptures reflected this. The Epistle was a humorous one. (Acts 19:13-17) A Jewish man was attempting to cast out a demon "in the name of Jesus whom Paul preaches." The demon replied to the man, "I know Jesus, and I know Paul, but who are you?" *Gotcha!*

The Gospel was the story of Jesus raising the little girl from the dead, taking Peter, James and John with him when he went to her side.

The former Abbot preached the sermon. "When you go to pray for a great healing, in the ICU for instance, you must do what Jesus did, and take with you people who can stand against the evidence." *Wow!* Jesus and his disciples were able to walk through the mourners who were wailing outside the girl's home and go to her side, standing against the evidence, seeing her whole and healed. The little girl came back to life.

After Mass, we went to breakfast. We had decided to skip Harry's this morning and just go to Renate's for lunch. I was so glad. I wanted to read and journal most of the day. Renate's was only ten minutes away.

At noon, the four of us assembled at Coy's car for the trip to Renate's. She was offering homemade weisswurst that day. I ordered that, plus an order of her potato salad. I had Renate's Black Forest cake for dessert. Three layers of medium-dark chocolate cake with white frosting and cherries in between each of the layers. Cherries corralled inside a frosting fence on the top. Tender crumbs of cake pressed into the frosting on the sides. I could not eat it all, so I had Renate box the rest for later.

We rode back to the monastery in contented silence. BA asked me if we could walk up the mountain at four. I agreed. She would come to my room for me.

I spent the afternoon reading *Love is the Link*, an account of a family doctor's Near Death Experience when she was a child, and the effect it had on the rest of her life.

For her, love blossomed and everything she saw for the rest of her life was suffused with beauty and love. As I read, I began to think: *her experience and its effects are "better" than mine. I'd rather live in a cloud of love than in a constant struggle for forgiveness. Then: Oops, this is not prompt, ungrudging, absolute obedience to God's plan for my life.*

Years later, I meet the author, Pamela Kircher MD, at an NDE conference. She absolutely was the most loving person I have ever met. Love flowed out of every pore. She listened kindly to me. She reminded me that we all had what she called "home-sickness for heaven." It was incredible sitting with her for a few minutes; I felt changed by her loving kindness.

I lay down for a nap and awakened when BA tapped on my door. I let her in and splashed water on my face. I prepared a note for the door telling where we had gone. I found that I didn't worry about going up the mountain with Michael, a man, but I felt that BA and I were more vulnerable.

We both had on slacks and our "rattlesnake shoes." When Michael and I walked in the early morning, it was probably too cold for rattlesnakes to move. Now it was full afternoon and warm. I put on my white shirt and sailor hat against the sun and we set off.

BA did an amazing job of climbing up the jeep road. The Physical Wellness had given her great fitness. We chattered away like BFFs do. I shared with her that I was a survivor of clergy sex abuse. She stopped right where she was and took me into her arms in a tight hug.

When we got back we went to our own rooms. I taped the sign from my door into my journal and then wrote a while until the bell for Vespers. I joined BA and Michael in the back row, Coy our ever-present satellite at the row's end. Dinner was turkey meatloaf; good, but no match for Renate's food.

137

I called Sarah and we visited about our adventures. We prayed together for her back.

The Thursday night video was about the city of Jerusalem. It was fascinating. Such history there.

The best part was a segment about a Muslim family who had kept the key to one of the churches in Jerusalem for the last 500 years, opening it and closing it every day. It seems that Christian factions were always fighting about who "owned" it and it was decided to let the Muslims manage it.

I returned to my room after the video and ate the rest of Renate's cake. I listened to Sarah's tape, put her new photos on the wall and fell into bed. All of this healing was exhausting.

That night I dreamed of Father Bernie, the School Director. In the dream he said to me, "Die to self."

the young monk
rolls up his sleeves
to read the gospel

TWENTY

1995, Pecos Benedictine Monastery, Week III, Friday

I awakened with the dream of Father Bernie telling me to die to self on my mind. I looked forward to discussing it with Michael.

As I showered I examined the possibilities. *Is this about writing? Is it something about my marriage? About motherhood? Is it something else entirely?*

A quick glance at my alarm sent me scurrying along the hallway, fearing I was late. I arrived at the grandfather clock just as it sounded the hour.

My experiment with not wearing a watch was going fine, but I found that I was mooching off of other timepieces several times a day.

We stepped through the door into the cool morning air. The growing crescent moon was high and bright. We headed across Route 63 and up the jeep trail.

I told Michael about my dream and asked him what he thought it meant. Of course he asked me what I thought it meant. I raised my questions and we kicked it around for a while. We both ended up feeling that it was about the writing, to die to what I had thought the rest of my life would be like and to accept my new life as a writer-doctor.

Michael was pumped about the day's Feast: Martyrs of the Early Church. *I feel like a martyr for the faith myself, with what Father Michael did to me.*

We got back in plenty of time and returned to our rooms. I changed into my sandals and moved down the hall to the chapel. Coy and BA were already seated. Michael joined us after a few moments.

One of the songs we sang was *The Servant Song*. Michael whispered that he wanted that song at his ordination to the diaconate, 18 months hence.

The sermon was open mike. Coy spoke about his retirement in the next decade and his wish to be a "Servant Leader." Servant leaders encourage, support and enable others to develop their abilities and fulfill their potential... Newsflash! *You already are well on your way to servant leadership, brother.*

At breakfast we complimented Coy on his sermon. Classmates stopped by to praise his sermon and some to ask the title of the book he'd referenced: *Servant Leadership* by Robert Greenleaf.

Abbot Andrew taught another class on biblical patterns and how we might find persons in the bible to identify with.

Sign me up! I am THERE with Job and Jeremiah. Those dudes were world-class whiners and moaners. No matter how much I complain, I could never compete with their individual abilities in that arena.

I really liked the Abbot's talk. I was able to listen fully even though I was stitching on Sarah's quilt.

Father Sam, a kindly monk who had been a Benedictine for 40 years, spoke next. He began with a bible verse, Ex. 34:7, "the sins of the fathers shall be visited upon the children and the children's children to the third and fourth generations."

Sam said that we would study some of the ways that those who have gone before us might have influenced us, even across generations. He said that he would celebrate tomorrow's private Mass for the School, with the intention of freeing us from these bondages.

He handed out blank genograms, where we might draw our family trees and a list of the various types of persons in our families, living or dead, who might need our prayers to free them and us from these bondages.

He invited us to list those in our families who were cut off, alienated, unloved and difficult. I scribbled down a few names.

Mother Teresa in her 1984 address to the Harvard graduating class said that the greatest poverty in the world is here in the U.S., a poverty of love. *"There is a terrible hunger for love...the poor you may have in your own family. Find them. Love them."*

I thought of my own family. Certainly each of us had some traits that made us unpopular in the larger group, but by and large, each of us was respectful to babies, announcing that we were about to move the stroller before we did so; the family went as slow as the slowest person.

Sam suggested adding childhood deaths. My brother, Jimmy, had died when Mother was pregnant with me. I put him on the list.

He suggested adding alcoholics or other addicts. Certainly my Dad and Father Michael drank. Together. I wondered what part this played in the sexual abuse of me, in Dad's "allowing" it, in Father Michael's doing it. I read somewhere that 50% of alcohol families are incest families. *Does the alcohol interfere with moral reasoning? Duh!* I wrote down both of their names.

Sam encouraged us to add the mentally ill, so that we might see their sickness and have compassion on them. I added a few more names. He asked us to add those we need to forgive and those we need to ask for forgiveness. No problem finding some names there!

He asked us to pray over this list over the next 24 hours, add to it if needed, and to bring it to the Saturday School Eucharist where we would release the persons to Christ and then burn the list as a symbol of this.

Sam also asked us to find a small rock somewhere on the grounds and to bring it Saturday to place on the altar. It would symbolize our family burdens and we would leave our rocks behind on the altar. Sam would carry them away, as Jesus had carried away our sins. He would drop the rocks in the river from the bridge so that all of the evil would be washed downriver.

I hope southern New Mexico and Texas don't mind....

Lunch was quiet, each of us thinking about the shadow side of our families. Turkey sloppy joes.

After lunch, I went to my room to get my scissors. I'd agreed to do the flower arrangements for the School Eucharist. The Sister Sacristan had liked the ones I had done last week and asked me to make new ones Friday afternoon so they could be up all weekend.

I walked the loop around the grounds watching for likely grasses. I found several more grasses in bloom, and several colors of fluffy, hundreds-on-a-stem flowers. I cut some upright grasses and more of the yellow flowers from last week, and the new ones in red, orange and purple. All of the flowers were approximately of the same density as baby's breath.

I went to the sacristy and made the arrangements. I put the grasses in back and created a "rainbow" in the front: red, orange, yellow, purple. It pleased me to do this, the rainbow being a symbol of God's covenant with us. And hope for the future.

Then it was time for Small Group. We began with progress reports and prayer requests. We discussed the topic for the day, the "Use of Scripture, Silence, and Sacred Symbols in Spiritual Direction."

Our discussion of our topic began with a discussion of Scripture itself. We debated whether we digest Scripture or whether it digests us. I shared that at home I had a few lines from Ephesians 6, "the armor of God," on the outside of my shower. I had read it every day for ten years and it was "new every morning"; the Spirit spoke to me about these few verses in a different way each day.

Someone remarked that this was the charismatic dimension of interaction with Scripture. The Spirit shows us the wisdom to be extracted from Scripture and then helps us figure out what to do with it.

We turned to the use of sacred symbols during Spiritual Direction. Some hung a cross or crucifix on the wall of the room where they directed. Some lit a votive candle as a sign the Spirit was the true Spiritual Director and the Spirit was present in each session. Someone said that symbols bridge two dimensions: body and spirit.

Time for my own Spiritual Direction. I spoke with Sister Debbie about my dream of Bernie's saying to me, "Die to self." She agreed with my sense that it was about becoming a writer. I showed her what I'd written about my family tree. She suggested adding the "left shoes" in my family, including myself, to the list.

Afterward Ann and BA and I walked around the grounds, chatting, until the Vespers bell sounded. Each of us had been hard at work on their list for the service the next day.

Dinner was turkey meatloaf, one of my favorites, with the ubiquitous mixed vegetables and a baked potato. In spite of my hearty eating, I was still losing weight; my khakis were getting very loose.

I called Sarah and we prayed together for her back. She'd gotten a big kick out of the card and letter I'd left for today: instructions on how to become a wacky, artistic woman.

The evening class was Abbot David speaking more about the development of the spirit through the spiritual disciplines. "The spiritual disciplines are two-handled tools. One handle for you, one for God. Don't forget to ask God to help you with keeping the disciplines." *I never thought of that. I guess I was raised to think I had to do all of that on my own.*

We had a short break before Prayer Ministry and Compline. During the service I went to Father Paul and asked for prayer to open my mind about who in my family I should pray for. No one new came to mind during the prayer. *Prayer is funny like that; sometimes it knocks you out with its power, sometimes feels like nothing special, but it heals you slowly, quietly and secretly.*

I returned to my room afterwards and listened to Sarah's tape. I put her photos on the wall and changed into nightclothes, and climbed into bed to read for a bit. Within five minutes I was exhausted. I turned out the light and fell asleep as soon as my head touched the pillow.

delicate flower petals
riding white waters
unscathed

TWENTY ONE

1995, Pecos Benedictine Monastery, Week III, Saturday

Friday night at dinner Michael said that he wanted to sleep in with the rest of the School on Saturday mornings from here on out. I quite understood. I asked BA to check before breakfast to make sure that I had made it back down the mountain safely.

At six a.m. I was ready to hike. I taped a note on my door saying that I was going up the jeep trail and would be back by 7.

I left the guesthouse at six through the side door near my room, first pushing open the heavy glass door, two steps on the enclosed concrete pad, then out a storm door.

I crossed Highway 63 and headed up the trail alone. The first part was easy, but when I approached the gate to the cattle ranch the dogs barked wildly and set my heart to pounding. Fortunately, the dogs did not approach the gate.

I followed the trail to the left and climbed to the moaning pine, keeping a good pace. It was not a particularly "spiritual" walk, as I was so anxious about the dogs and about "something bad" happening to me up there on the trail alone. I feared turning my ankle and having to lie there until someone came. Or crimes against my person.

I paused for a moment to admire the waxing moon and headed back down the mountain at a good clip.

As I reentered the monastery grounds I began to look for a rock for the service. I found a heart-shaped one in the gravel and dropped it into my pocket.

I returned to my room and pulled the note from my door, taping it into my notebook. I kicked off my sneakers and slipped on my Birks; I sat on the bed waiting for the bell before leaving for the chapel area.

I slid into the tiny room off of the chapel and closed the door silently. I took up my prayer position, leaning against the wall, one hand on each side of the chalice mosaic. I could hear the Community singing off and on and chanting psalms, but no clear words came through the wall.

When I heard them leave the chapel through the sacristy, I left the consultation room and headed down the hall to the classroom. I sat in my chair in the faint warmth of the early morning sunbeam.

Soon I heard my classmates heading toward me. BA sat down in the chair beside me and gave me a side hug. She'd gone by my room, as promised, to make sure I was back. When she saw that I'd taken the note down, she knew I was safe.

The dining room gong sounded and we all trooped upstairs for breakfast. Huge hot, home-baked biscuits! I took two, a slab of butter and a runny, dark gob of blackberry jam. And a big glass of milk. BA and I sat down at one of the octagonal tables. A grouchy man, a visitor, sat with us.

When we finished our breakfasts, BA and I headed downstairs.

Father Paul was standing quietly at the front, waiting for the class. After we settled, he spoke about the Spirituality of Middle Life. A depression can come on in mid-life if a person has not adequately spiritualized his life. Many people, he said, become suicidal if they do not believe in an afterlife by the time they turn 50.

He reminded us that the service we give to the world comes naturally out of our gifts and out of our spiritual maturation. This service, he said, must be something that we love.

I felt my shoulders slump into deep relaxation, calm and relief. I guess that I always figured that my service would have to be something that I hated, an odious "growth experience."

Paul spoke of the two book reports due next summer as a requirement for graduation. He reminded us that we could report on any topic covered in the School; any book in the bookstore; or any book on Spiritual Direction.

Abbot David gave the next class. His lecture was about prayer and how getting the body involved in prayer could be helpful. This might be as simple as bowing your head, or raising your face "to the light." It might be raising your hands, clapping or swaying. These body movements, the Abbot said, help us to avoid distraction and help us to focus on God's presence in the moment.

I'll bow my head; I'll lift my face; I'll raise my hands; I'll sway, but I still hate clapping.

Later Abbot David said an amazing thing, "the inner child is bigger than the ego." This was exactly what I was sensing with my right-hand/ left-hand dialogs. I never would have trusted my own experience.

The self that I access with the dialogs is so wise. She sees right into the heart of things. She is non-judgmental and kind. And she knows Jesus. I realized with a start that all of these things were true of my so-called-retarded brother, Peter. "The inner child is bigger than the ego"...I'd known Peter for forty years had yet to see much sign of "ego" in him.

After class there was plenty of time before lunch. I returned to my room to dialog with my "inner child who was bigger than my ego." Purple and green pens again.

Me: That man at breakfast scared me! He was so angry and confrontational. I felt so angry at him.

Little me: I was angry, too.

Me: I probably misquoted something but I didn't like him coming after me like that.

Little me: He was mean.

Me: He scares people because he is scared?

Little me: Approval is so important to him.

Me: Do we do that to Sarah?

Little me: Sometimes.

Me: Sarah's dad?

Little me: Yes.

Me: Who treated you like that?

Little me: Mom and Dad. Mom's mother was so unpredictable that it was better for her to be good. Dad was so naughty when he was a boy that he was always afraid.

Jesus says be little children, but you make Sarah be so big in church.

Me: So maybe I should let her be a baby in church?

Little me: Yes.

Me: Is that why I cry in church?

Little me: Yes.

Me: I feel like a baby?

Little me: Yes. Jesus likes babies.

Me: What do you need?

Little me: Quiet. Nature. Hugs.

Me: I love you.

Little me: I love you.

I reread the dialog. Wow again. My inner child definitely WAS bigger than my ego. Abbot David was right on. And I needed to think more about my so-called-retarded brother.

I lay down to process this. All of this personal growth was exhausting!

I fell asleep, awakening when the bell called us to the School's private Eucharist. I splashed water on my face, grabbed my list of family members "in bondage to sin," checked my pocket for my rock and sped down the hall.

As I entered the chapel, I saw the famous plastic trash can, the one for Kleenex, right by the door.

I was the last of the "four amigos" to arrive in our row. The Sister Sacristan had placed my rainbow flower arrangements on either side of the altar.

Father Sam was waiting in front of the altar, already vested, a compassionate smile on his face. He explained the liturgy to come. First we would sing, then the Scripture reading and sermon then the placing of the rocks and lists on the altar, then the Passing of the Peace, then Communion with more singing. He reminded us of the box of Kleenex beneath each chair.

We started with *Ubi Caritas*, a song in Spanish that is about love being everywhere.

Sam read the Gospel, the story of Jesus traveling in Samaria, to the north of Judea and stopping at Jacob's well at midday. The only person about was the Samaritan woman, who was drawing water from the 135-foot deep well.

Sam read so compassionately that I was crying already; I was not the only one. Jesus asked her for water, i.e., He spoke to someone regarded as "not of the faith" and asked her to comfort him. He instructed her about a never-ending source of refreshment, living water, a source available to all; and told her that he was the Messiah. I was sobbing openly by now. Others were, too.

Sam began to preach. He told how at one time Samaria and Judah were one nation of Jews, but fighting broke out between two huge factions and the Jews of Jesus' group no longer recognized the Samaritans as "true Jews."

Jesus, Sam said, made it clear in his teaching that He was here to bring living water, a deep, fathomless well of grace to refresh our parched souls. Our souls would be refreshed whether they were parched from our own sin or whether they were parched from sin committed against us.

Jesus made it clear, Sam said, that He was here for all, not just the "converted." I thought of that stupid cartoon in the break room and its reference to "choosing the right religion."

I thought of Costanzo referring to me as a "fallen Catholic." Sam spoke directly to this: if we followed Jesus of Nazareth, we were Christians. Period. And if we followed Jesus of Nazareth, we were welcome at the Lord's Table.

He invited us forward to place our rocks, representing the burden of sin in ourselves and our families, on the altar. More quiet sobs all through the chapel.

We filed forward. I laid the heart-shaped rock on a heavy platter on the left side of the altar and returned to my seat.

Then he asked us to come forward again with the lists of our family members who needed prayer. He cautioned us to add ourselves before coming up if we were not on the list already. More sobs. More people clutching damp wads of Kleenex as they came forward to place their lists on the altar.

We passed the Peace; Sam participated, but carefully watched each of us to see if we were OK.

We moved into the Communion portion of the service. Sam offered our rocks up, lifting the plate that they rested on. He held up our lists also, praying over them at length, asking for healing in us and our families. More sobs.

Then he prayed the usual prayers over the bread and wine.

He stepped before the altar with the bread and wine. A female classmate came and took the wine from him. He told us that we had left our burdens behind on the altar; we should leave them there. He gave us the bread from his own hands and our classmate, a Baptist, gave us the wine. Clearly he meant what he had said about the oneness of all Christians.

We took our seats again.

Father Paul, dressed in his white robes, entered the chapel carrying a huge wok. The two monks bowed to one another. They put the papers with our family members needing prayer into the wok and covered them with a wire mesh lid. They asked us to follow them outside. Coy held open the door to the chapel.

I grabbed a fresh handful of dry tissues and dropped my wet Kleenex into the trash can. I was pretty sure that the crying was not over yet.

The priests led us to the door facing the river. We walked across the grass to the stone altar overlooking the fields and the Pecos River. The priests set the lists aflame. We watched as the smoke ascended to the heavens, taking our burdens with it. More sobs.

The two monks bowed to one another again. Paul left, taking the wok with him.

Sam stood in front of the stone altar and led us in singing *On Eagle's Wings*. Many leaking eyes.

When we finished the song, he dismissed us, reminding us that he was leaving to drop our rocks in the river, allowing the Pecos to carry away our pain and our family's pain. He took up the platter and set off toward the river.

There was another trashcan just outside of the door to the guesthouse. We dropped our new wet Kleenex into it.

BA and I walked along the long corridor of the guesthouse towards her room. Once there we turned and looked out the window. We watched Sam in his white robes carrying the tray of rocks down towards the river.

I bade BA a hasty goodbye and moved along the short corridor connecting her hallway and mine. I was whipped and wanted to lie down. I was sure I would sleep; I was right.

The bell for Vespers awakened me. I splashed water on my face and stumbled along the hall to the chapel for singing and psalms.

Dinner was turkey meatballs on noodles with salad. We were a subdued group that evening.

I called Sarah and was enlivened by her cheerful voice. We prayed together for her back.

The evening class was given by Sister Miriam. She spoke on the Jungian concept of Shadow. Shadow is the place where we put all of the parts of ourselves we do not want to own or those for which we wish to blame others.

Typically, the shadow is unconscious and thus unavailable for conscious processing by the mind.

True freedom, Miriam said, comes from knowing the Shadow and having it become part of the conscious mind. This, she said, allows us to exert considerable control over its impulses.

Solitude, with self-examination, i.e., asking what did I do, and why in the world did I do it? Journaling. Confession. Spiritual Direction. These are all ways of making the Shadow more conscious and accessible to free will.

Character change can come from the embrace of the Shadow.

Wow. That is why my relationship with my Spiritual Director / Confessor is so powerful, so healing.

My routine involved my daily three-mile walks at dawn, solitude; journaling through the month; keeping track of my sins; an examination of my spiritual progress and confession of my backsliding during a two hour meeting with her each month. (Note: Therapy and Small Group can also help to make unconscious motivation conscious)

When Miriam dismissed us, I sped down the hall. I was beyond tired. I changed into my PJs, turned off the light and fell asleep. I was so tired that I forgot to listen to Sarah's tape.

blushing faintly
three windfall apples
in the cart track

TWENTY TWO

1995, Pecos Benedictine Monastery, Week IV, Sunday

I awakened before the alarm, sat up and pressed down the switch. Our last Sunday here! Michael would be joining me on my walk. I got ready and stepped silently down the hall to the clock, arriving just a moment before Michael. We were unusually quiet on the uphill that morning, perhaps because of the emotions stirred up by the service the afternoon before.

We stood in the dawn breeze beside the moaning pine. The pine made no pretense of keeping its emotions to itself, moaning earnestly in the wind.

Our chat was desultory on the way down, mostly about our final visits of the year to Harry's and Renate's later today. We parted when we got back to the residence.

I pushed off my sneakers; I never untie them. I slipped on my Birks. I listened to Sarah's tape, which she had meant for the night before, and stuck her photos to the wall.

When the bell called me to chapel, I moved along the hallway, arriving first in "our pew." The Praise songs were excellent, as I had come to expect and enjoy.

Two Community members were leaving on a short mission trip. The Abbot had them come forward and prayed Psalm 91, a prayer of protection, over them.

The Eucharist was uplifting and satisfying.

We returned to our rooms, making no pretense of eating breakfast on site, and regrouped at Coy's car, outside the glass doors of the residence. Girls in the back, boys in the front.

At Harry's I had fresh squeezed orange juice, blue cornmeal waffles with honey butter, and a side of bacon. We passed on dessert in anticipation of our visit to Renate's later.

When we arrived in Santa Fe we parked at the Inn at Loreto again. On the way to the square, we paused at the table that my favorite Indian jeweler, Nestor Tenorio, had set up outside the Chapel at Loreto. My eyes caressed the lyrical lines of his jewelry; a faint smile creased my face. I looked up and smiled into his eyes, acknowledging my pleasure at seeing his work again.

Looking ahead to the square, we saw that there was quite a crowd, so we split into pairs and agreed to meet back at the car at noon. Thankfully BA had on her Mickey Mouse watch, as I was still watchless.

When we got to San Francisco Street, we saw that there was a procession; this was the cause of the huge crowd. We were lucky enough to get there just as it got underway.

First came a large group of people in period Spanish dress. These were followed by many little girls in their lacy white First Communion dresses and veils. The girls carried white baskets of pink rose petals, which they strewed on the street.

The girls were followed by a group of four men carrying a wooden statue of Mary on a pallet. Around the wooden statue were pink roses, matching the rose petals the little girls were strewing.

These four men and the twenty other men who surrounded them all wore black trousers, wide red pleated belts, and white dress shirts. Each had a yellow and red ribbon around his neck with a large dangling gold medallion.

The parishioners of the cathedral parish followed, all dressed in black, the younger women helping their elderly mothers.

At the end of the procession was the Archbishop. He wore his miter on his head and carried his shepherd's crook. He was surrounded by a dozen of his priests.

Later I would learn that the statue carried in the procession is the oldest Madonna statue in the Americas, dating to 1625.

When the procession had passed, BA and I proceeded to the square where we did what all red-blooded American women do: we browsed.

I was especially moved by paintings in one of the galleries on the square. They had unusual tiny highlights that seemed to be created with florescent paint. I was especially taken by one painting of the full moon. Some of its craters had miniscule dots of glowing paint on their rims.

As we moved about the shops on the square, we touched things, we exclaimed, but neither of us bought anything. We visited the Palace of the Governors where Native Americans displayed jewelry on blankets on the ground.

We looked with great interest, but again, bought nothing. Consulting BA's watch, we saw it was almost noon, so we hurried back to the car.

The guys were waiting. They said that they had seen the procession and had enjoyed the spectacle. It was all new to Coy, who had never had much to do with Catholics before.

We rode to Renate's in companionable, expectant silence.

I asked Renate to bring the dessert menu with the lunch menu so that I could plan my meal carefully. I chose a smoked filet of trout with creamy horseradish sauce and a tangy side of red cabbage. For dessert I ordered Renate's Waldberen torte: vanilla sponge cake with fresh berries: strawberries, blackberries, raspberries and blueberries, all caulked together with stiffly-whipped cream. More whipped cream covered the cake and was piped around the edges of the dessert. Divine.

When I got back to my room, I journaled about the procession. Then I took a ceremonial Sunday afternoon nap, something I love to do at home. When I awakened, I lay back on the bed and looked at the ceiling. Looking at the ceiling was something that I'd learned to do in med school to relieve stress and get back to baseline.

Later, when I got my faith back, I'd learned about keeping the Sabbath in order to get back to baseline. I'd kept a pretty good Sabbath for eight years by the time I went to Pecos.

In a Bible Study I'd read the Ten Commandments in Exodus and had noted that the Sabbath Commandment takes up 40% of the lines. I'd realized keeping the Sabbath must be pretty important.

I found keeping the Sabbath got my body, mind and spirit back to the baseline that the "manufacturer" intended.

That Sunday afternoon at the monastery, I lay on my back for about an hour. My eyes traced patterns in the knotty pine of the ceiling.

When the Vespers bell rang, I splashed water on my face and brushed my teeth, then slipped on my Birks and walked to the chapel.

The Praise and psalms were uplifting. Afterward we moved to the classroom and then, at the sounding of the gong, up to the dining room.

Turkey Salisbury steak. Tasty, but not in the same league as Harry's or Renate's.

I called Sarah after dinner.

BA waited in the classroom while I called, then we loaded up on graham crackers and headed for the duck pond. I spoke with BA about the way I kept Sabbath and how much it helped me. She was intrigued. She liked to plant and tend her flowers on Sunday and wondered if that was "allowed."

I suggested that she read the Ten Commandments in Exodus and pray about it, God always being the ultimate source of information about keeping His laws. We fed the ducks, and then sat on the bench for some time, talking. Afterwards we walked one circuit of the grounds.

I skipped the video that night and read. When I was tired I listened to Sarah's tape and puttied her photos to the wall, and fell into a contented sleep.

the waft of woodsmoke
from my clothes
remembering lunch out

TWENTY THREE

1995, Pecos Benedictine Monastery, Week IV, Monday

My eyes popped open before the alarm. I lay there enjoying the soft dawn light, and then sat up to turn off the alarm before it could chirp.

I read the syllabus, and got ready for the day. Just before six I shoved my feet into my sneakers, bending the back flap forward before inserting my finger to wriggle the tab back upright.

I hurried down the hall, where Michael was waiting by the clock. It sounded the hour as I arrived. We pushed open the heavy wooden door, carved with a descending dove, and stepped into the cool morning air.

As we headed up the jeep trail "paved" with jagged rock I told Michael of a trip my family had taken to the Big Island of Hawaii.

I had hired an archeologist to take us out into the petroglyph fields. The archeologist took us early in the morning when the slanting rays of the sun best exposed the carvings in the flat lava flows.

He showed us carvings in the golden-tan lava where Hawaiians had chipped circles when dedicating their children to the gods. The natives would leave the child's umbilical cord in the circle. There was a surprising but definite feeling of "church" in these places. The archeologist showed me other places that recorded journeys but there was no feeling of "church" in those places.

He showed me the "King's Highway," a path through the lava flows. The King's Highway circled the island, creating trade access between the pie-shaped chiefdoms on the island.

I began to follow the path, which was very shallow, maybe a quarter inch. It was hip-wide and carved by the bare feet of the natives. Walking on it was the "best possible path" through the lava, even though it doubled back frequently. The few times that

I tried stepping over a sharp turn in the path, trusting myself rather than the well-worn path, I immediately twisted my ankle. I soon realized that the best way to follow this path was to surrender to the wisdom of those who had gone before.

I noticed a stick-straight path at a little distance. It was bordered in long, carved rectangular stones and filled with sharp-edged rubble. "Oh, that is the missionary's path," the archeologist said. "They rode their mules on that."

I walked over and tried it. I turned my ankle at every step. Michael laughed. We were at a charismatic monastery and were very much attuned to finding the "right path," even though it might be a bit crooked or a bit curvier than that directed by the average missionary. Or by his mule.

We paused by the moaning pine for a few moments and looked out at the Pecos Valley.

Then we headed back. We arrived in plenty of time to go to our rooms and, for me, to change shoes. I zigged and zagged down my hallway to the chapel, running into Michael who was hurrying down the main corridor.

We took our places beside BA. After our exhilarating walk, the Praise songs were very powerful. Passing the peace was gratifying.

We had a jolly breakfast and afterward came downstairs to see Sister Theresa waiting for us. Thankfully the lights were on. No crying today.

Her topic was prayer. Interestingly, she spoke of Psalm 23 (The Lord is my shepherd ...) and that it was, in many ways, a prayer of the inner child. She read from the Good News Version of the bible. "He guides me on right paths, as he has promised."

Just like the King's Highway, the right path may not be the obvious path but if I surrender and allow Him to guide me, I will always be on the right path. And just like the King's Highway in Hawaii, the right path is crooked, meandering, and nothing like the missionary's path.

Brother Matt was next. He spoke of prayer also. Prayer, he said, unites us more to God and to our neighbor. If we experience God's love for us through prayer, we naturally "get" how much

God loves our neighbor. This suddenly shed light on that mysterious command "Love your neighbor as yourself." *If I am fully aware of God's intense love for me, I will love me, too. And I will love my neighbor. Pretty cool.*

I returned to my room to read before lunch. When I heard the bell, I scurried along the hallway to the classroom and waited with the others for the dining room gong.

Asian turkey salad with buns and a side salad.

We were still upbeat. No one had made us cry in at least a day.

BA wanted to skip Physical Wellness and walk with me, so I agreed to knock on her door at 2:30 p.m. and we would go on a walk on the grounds.

I returned to my room to read and nap a little. My alarm woke me and I splashed water on my face, brushed my teeth again and hurried through the pass-thru hall between BA's hallway and mine.

I knocked lightly on her door and she opened it immediately, sweeping me into a big hug. We slipped out the river door and walked behind the cloister to the dirt road. We passed the cottage where Rick and Penny were staying. They were on the schedule to lecture to us tonight.

Continuing down the road, we headed for the duck pond. I had graham crackers in my pocket, so we stopped to feed the growing ducklings.

We continued along the river road, jabbering away. We noted the faint purpling of the baby grapes on a fence along the river road.

We spoke of Rick and Penny's upcoming talk about marriage that night. We spoke of our marriages and our hopes for them. We took the path to the falls and sat beside them for a long time, talking and listening to the water splash.

We returned to the circle path and finished the circuit, noting the deepening red on the apples in the orchard.

We parted at the far entrance of the residence, BA turning toward her hallway, facing the river, I continuing along my hallway, facing the road and the sun.

I stopped to admire the curved "adobe" walls of my hallway, the pattern of light and shadow and the beautiful golden-tan color on the walls.

I read and journaled until the Vespers bell. I tromped down the hall to the chapel where BA and Michael were already seated. Coy was at the end of the row, as usual.

Wonderful Praise songs and psalms. Then it was time for dinner. Turkey meatballs and buttered noodles with poppy seeds. Those same mixed vegetables: broccoli, cauliflower and carrots. Good, but not fine dining.

Time to call Sarah and to pray with her. She was so happy to hear my voice. I did not like being away from my 12 year old for four weeks. She was happy and well cared for by Linda, and spent her days with her soul mate Robin but still....The girls had been born one hour apart in different states and had been tight since they met when they were five. They were probably friends in heaven before they came here. Robin's mom Linda and I had clicked on a preschool field trip with the girls.

The evening class was very different. Rick and Penny, resident Oblates married to one another, gave the talk on marriage.

They spoke of their calling to the vocation of marriage. How they had consulted God about whether the other was "the one" God had chosen for them. How they constantly relied on God to help them "do" marriage.

They had, they said, become an integral part of one another. Rick said that he'd become fully male by nurturing Penny and the kids; Penny said she'd become fully female by nurturing Rick and their kids. They were, they said, fully ready to lay down their lives for one another.

In difficult times they went to the Blessed Mother and said, "I have no wine in my marriage, I need new wine."

Something clicked deep inside of me when Penny said that. Suddenly the Blessed Mother was THERE for me again. And suddenly I saw my home with a gallon jug of red wine on each of the steps leading to the second floor. *Wow. That is a lavish amount of wine. I couldn't drink that much in my lifetime!*

One thing Penny said troubled me. She said that she submitted to Rick's headship. I resolved to speak to Michael about it in the morning.

The talk had stirred up my classmates to a quiet buzz. I stayed and visited a bit before going to my room to reading and getting ready for bed. I lay my head on the pillow and fell into a confused sleep.

hip wide
carved by human soles
the King's Highway

TWENTY FOUR

1995, Pecos Benedictine Monastery, Week IV, Tuesday, July 4

I awoke before the alarm and lay there enjoying the peace of the morning and the lack of need to hurry. I arose and got ready for the day. At six I stepped quickly and lightly down the hall and waited by the clock for Michael. I could see him coming along the long hallway.

We pushed open the heavy door and stepped into the cool morning air.

On the way uphill I asked for his thoughts about Penny's statement the night before about Rick's "headship." Of course Michael asked me what I thought before speaking. I told him that I struggled with the concept of headship.

Michael said that the position of the church was shifting on headship. Men and women, more and more, are seen as equal partners in marriage. *That feels so right to me!*

I told Michael as much. I told him that the marriage promises Sarah's dad and I had written were promises made by co-equals. The woman judge who performed the ceremony tacked on the standard "love, honor, cherish, in sickness and in health" language. Nowhere was language that was unequal.

We talked about the day to come. Although it was a Tuesday, the Thursday schedule prevailed because of the Fourth of July holiday. We would have no class. The four amigos had decided to stay on the monastery grounds and "soak it up" before our departure next Sunday.

We returned to the guesthouse and parted to get ready for morning Praise and Eucharist. When I slid into the pew a few minutes later, Coy was already in place at the end of the row, in the corner. I realized that he had been there early every single day; likely getting in his morning prayer time. *I'm quick!* BA and

Michael arrived soon after. I had heard them sharing a laugh just before they came in.

We made a joyful noise and then had the Lord's Supper with a warm and comforting Passing of the Peace.

Breakfast was marked with joy and hilarity. I added a saucer of nunsuch banana to my usual bowl of cereal.

BA and I decided to walk after breakfast. We circled the grounds three times talking about the marriage material that had been presented the night before.

We decided that we would renew our marriage vows. On our third circuit, we picked wildflowers for our bouquets from the edge of the dirt road.

We stopped in BA's room to pick up her *Book of Common Prayer*, the Episcopal Church's book containing prayers and the liturgies for all of the major services.

We took our bouquets and sat on the short stone wall near the hollyhocks that had figured in the hollyhock wedding. BA acted as minister; I clutched my bouquet tightly as she led me through my marriage vows.

Then BA handed me the Prayer Book and took up her bouquet. I laid my bouquet on the wall beside me and led BA through her marriage vows. We grinned at each other; the renewal felt good.

I returned to my room and pressed my bouquet flat in my red spiral notebook and weighted it with books. The bouquet had daisies, sprays of small white flowers, and three kinds of small purple flowers, including violets.

I read until the lunch bell. We had turkey meatballs on hot-dog buns, and salad.

BA and I walked again after lunch. Afterward I returned to my room and read some more. I reread my journal from the beginning, taking care not to disturb my flattened bouquet.

The smell of hot charcoal briquettes began to fill the air.

The Vespers bell rang and I made my way to the chapel for Praise and psalms.

Then we all exited the chapel and went out the door by the grandfather clock. We circled around to the right past the classroom and the break room until we got to the carport area.

Brother Matt was laying Polish sausages and hamburgers on the grill, made of actual pork and actual beef. *Woohoo.*

We stood around in small clumps watching and chatting. Soon the meat was ready; we lined up to fill our plates with homemade potato salad, homemade cole slaw, meat and buns. We grabbed sodas, the first we had seen at the monastery.

We four amigos carried our plates riverward to a spot beside the laughing brook. We sat in the grass to enjoy our food and one other.

After dinner, the four of us disposed of our trash and walked a loop around the grounds. When we got back I went to call Sarah. The others returned to their rooms.

The bell called us to Compline with its singing and psalms. As the sun set, we headed outside through the river door.

The monks had set up rows of chairs so we could watch the fireworks. It was chilly, so I asked BA to save my seat and ran inside for a sweater.

Brother Matt, in his absolute, unquestioning obedience to the Abbot, was assembling the fireworks on the outdoor stone altar. When the Abbot gave the signal, Matt began to set them off, one by one. Booms were followed by trails in the sky or giant flowers of light.

When these were done, Matt handed two sparklers to each of us. We lit them and horsed around like a bunch of kids swinging our arms in circles. Our energetic Baptist preacher ran wildly though the group, bent over with a sparkler by each ear.

When our sparklers were spent, BA and I stepped toward the nuns' dorm where we could see the huge New Mexico stars, each one appearing larger and closer than any stars I have seen before or since. We returned to our rooms.

What a wonderful day! I read for a bit and then fell into bed in happy exhaustion.

July 4
the first patch
of little bluestem

TWENTY FIVE

1995, Pecos Benedictine Monastery, Week IV, Wednesday

My internal alarm was working perfectly. I awakened before my alarm sounded. I lay there enjoying the sounds of the birds, then arose and clicked off the alarm.

I got ready, shoved on my sneakers and quietly hurried down the hall to meet Michael. He was beside the clock already waiting in his humble Benedictine stance. I pushed open the heavy door and we stepped out into the cool air.

We spoke of the thoroughly enjoyable day we'd had the day before. Michael was pumped about going to the Mother House of the religious order he was about to join.

It was amazing how fit we'd become climbing that mountain every day. We were breathing normally when we reached the top. We walked down the mountain quickly and arrived back at the guesthouse in plenty of time to change shoes.

Coy was in the pew when I arrived in the chapel. He nodded quietly to me. BA was next to arrive and then Michael. Soon the Praise music began; our spirits and voices soared beyond the celestial blue tiles of the ceiling. Passing the Peace to 60+ people was wonderful. Ann gave the sermon, a good one about trusting God.

Breakfast was very joyful. Ann ate with us. All through breakfast classmates and monastics came up to congratulate her on her sermon. I made her a nunsuch banana to celebrate her accomplishment.

Abbot Andrew gave both classes in the morning. He spoke of the New Age Movement, whose Gnostic roots go back to pre-Christianity.

What I took away from his talks is that God is a person, not a cosmic vending machine. We interact with the Person of God.

His bottom line was that Jesus is the only intermediary we need in intercessory prayer.

As I stitched on my quilt block my mind wandered *I am all over interceding through Jesus, but it was not always that way for me. It was science that brought me back to God.*

My first adult perception of God was of God as Creator as I studied the human body in med school.

About six years later I began to apprehend the help of the Holy Spirit in working with my patients in therapy.

Jesus was still very frightening and "other" to me. I remember listening to a tape where you were to ask for a spirit guide and the guide who arrived was Jesus. I immediately shut off the tape, jumped up off of the couch and left the room.

Years later I found that tape and it was still stopped just at that spot. I know I must have had Jesus all muddled up with Father Michael.

Listening to the Abbot, I mused about all of the un-churched or de-churched people and wondered about what trauma had happened to them to make them leave. Listening to him I wanted to say that sometimes a person just can't go through Jesus to start with, through no fault of their own.

Abbot Andrew said that the New Age Movement flourishes whenever the Gospel is preached as "words" without acts of love and caring.

Duh! When church leaders transfer known pedophiles to new assignments where they can rape other children, there is a distinct failure of love and caring.

After class BA and Ann and I walked around the grounds. We spoke mostly of our daughters, and in BA's case, granddaughters as well. I returned to my room to rest and read. The bell summoned me to lunch.

Lunch was leftover meatballs from yesterday's lunch and sausages and hamburgers from the cookout. I heaped my plate with real pork and beef. I sat with the other amigos. A monk offered grace. Michael, the eternal comic, muttered "no need to bless it, it's leftovers."

After lunch I returned to my room to read, journal and do a right-hand/ left-hand dialog.

Purple and green again.

Me: It was so nice to be treated kindly here.

Little me: Yes.

Me: We have our real self brought out.

Little me: Yes.

Me: Now we have to extend that into the real world.

Little me: Yes.

Me: Yuck.

Little me: Yes.

Me: I will with God's help. (Note: This phrase is used five times in the Episcopal *Renewal of Baptism* vows.)

Little me: Yes.

Me: Do you need anything?

Little me: Quiet. Naps. Pack.

Me: You need quiet, solitude, naps and to be all packed.

Little me: Yes.

After journaling I felt perfectly well.

At 2:30, I stopped by BAs room, as requested, to get her for our walk. We exited through the heavy wooden front door: I trailed the fingers of my left hand over the carved dove as I pushed it open with my right hand.

We headed toward the gift shop with its nearby cottonwood. I invited BA to stand with me under the tree and listen to its incomparable crescendo/ decrescendo of leaf flutter in the wind.

On my walks at home, I always paused under a massive cottonwood to listen to its leaves.

We headed toward the dirt road. Passing Rick and Penny's cabin had a lot more meaning to us now that they had taught us. Another cabin behind theirs was that of a Resident Oblate, but we never had any contact with her.

We proceeded to the duck pond where the "ducklings" were almost fully fledged with their adult colors; tufts of down peeking out here and there. Their maturity didn't stop them from begging for graham crackers. We gladly fed them.

We walked onto the bridge over the Pecos and watched the clear water slide along over smooth rocks.

I wonder if my "family" rock is still here near the bridge. I wonder if grace has washed us clean.

After a long time on the bridge, we meandered along the dirt road beside the river and up the trail to the falls. Again we sat there and chatted. *I surely wish this woman lived near me in Texas. We could be in daily contact.*

After a time we headed back to the residence, taking our time.

I napped until the Vespers bell, then splashed water on my face and brushed my teeth. BA and Michael were already in "our" pew, as was Coy. Wonderful singing and psalms said with joy and fervor.

At dinner we were back to Turkeyville: turkey meatloaf with mashed potatoes and those mixed vegetables. We stayed and chatted for a long time after dinner until a monk silently turned off the overheads in a quiet signal that the dining room was closed. Sarah was away with Robin so I was free to join my friends on a walk.

The four of us walked around the dirt road after dinner. Only BA was looking forward to our evening "Creative Movement" class with Sister Geralyn. After our walk, I returned to my room for a bit of rest and reading. I heard my classmates thumping down the hall. My alarm informed me that it was time for class.

Joyful, flexible Geralyn led us in some Liturgical Dance moves. Again BA excelled. Again Coy, Michael and I kept Benedictine reserve.

I was exhausted from the class. I hate stuff like that. I went to my room immediately to detoxify, read and get ready for bed.

noonday meal
no need to bless it
leftovers

TWENTY SIX

1995, Pecos Benedictine Monastery, Week IV, Thursday

My eyes popped open before my alarm went off. Four more days here.

I got ready and hurried silently down the hall, zigging right and zagging left. Again I arrived at the grandfather clock before Michael. As I turned to look down the long main corridor I could see him coming.

He pushed open the heavy door and we stepped out into the cool mountain air. We crossed the highway and headed up the jeep trail.

I felt a bit of that angry stomach ache that I'd felt the day before. I told Michael about my stomach and how the right-hand/ left-hand dialog had cleared it until now. "Maybe you can dialog again today," he said.

We paused at the moaning pine, and then headed back. We parted on entering the guesthouse.

I changed shoes and headed to chapel. *I wonder if watchless monks develop an internal alarm clock for the hours the bell will ring, calling them to worship, just like I wake up without my alarm now.* I resolved to ask Michael on our walk the next morning.

I have had a lot of wonderful worship experiences in the years since Pecos, but singing Praise songs after climbing a mountain trail has to rank up there among the best.

By now I had gotten to know quite a few of my classmates and passing the Peace to them was wonderful and warm. I approached each of the 60+ people with respect and caution, trying to sense the type of embrace the person needed that day, and each of them returned the same compassion.

Breakfast was a hoot. We sat down at a table with Abbot Andrew and Brother Matt. I sat beside the Abbot; Matt was on his other side. I decided to pull Matt's tail.

After the blessing, I asked Matt if he were a mime. He said that he wasn't. Eyes dancing, the Abbot asked me why I'd thought that about Matt. I replied that Matt had an extremely expressive face.

Matt's eyes began to dart around and he began to hyperventilate. Gulping air, Adam's apple bouncing, he explained that he'd come from a family of five and that his parents expected them to be silent at meals. The kids had learned to communicate by silent means. I said that he'd be a great mime.

He looked like he wanted to die. I know that he was thinking of the absolute, unquestioning obedience he had promised to the Abbot. The Abbot's eyes were twinkling, sensing this also. Soon, to Matt's obvious relief, the conversation moved to other topics.

Our first class was a talk about Spirituality by Abbot David. I was in such a mind meld with this Abbot that I rarely took notes when he spoke, but rather listened intently and stitched.

One thing that I wrote down that morning is worth revisiting. "Healing and growth come from hanging in the tension that comes from being outside of your comfort zone; and from making yourself present to God in that tension." *Wow! You could spend your whole life working on that one!*

Next was a talk by a nun who was also an RN, Sister Ann. She spoke of healthy nutrition: healthy fats, healthy choices in milk products, and the food pyramid. I put my head down and stitched. There was way too much healthy food at the monastery. Way too little joy in the food.

I did not then and do not now see food as simply fuel, but also as a source of the joy of the Lord. I got quite a few quilt squares done that morning! My stomach discomfort persisted, however, so I decided to slip out of Sister Ann's lecture early and go to my room to dialog.

The dialog that follows is an exact transcript of what my right hand and left hand wrote that morning. There are four "voices" in this dialog: Me, Little me, Jesus and Father Michael. At two points Jesus calls Father Michael "my Michael."

Me: My stomach is hurting again, as if I were angry. What's up?

Little me: I'm angry with Costanzo. I DIDN'T FALL, I WAS PUSHED!

Me: You are angry that Costanzo called you a fallen Catholic?

Little me: YES!

Me: He was pretty judgmental.

Little me: YES!

Me: How do you feel about being pushed?

Little me: Angry! I love God. I always did.

Me: Are you angry at Costanzo?

Little me: Yes, but I am angry at Father Michael, too.

Me: You are angry at Father Michael?

Little me: Yes.

Me: Can you say why?

Little me: Father Michael hurt me. He not like Jesus.

Me: When he raped you, he didn't act like Jesus.

Little me: Right.

Me. You know Jesus?

Little me: Yes. Nice man.

Me: Are you comfortable with Jesus?

Little me: Yes.

Me: Safe?

Little me: Yes.

Me: Father Michael lives with Jesus.

(long pause)

Me: You are surprised?

Little me: Yes.

Me: Father Michael is dead. He is in heaven.

Little me: Not hell?

Me: Jesus forgave him.

Little me: Oh.

Me: You are surprised?

Little me: Yes.

Me: Would you like to ask Jesus about it?

Little me: Yes.

Me: Jesus is here now.

Little me: Hello, Jesus. I am glad to see you.

Jesus: I'm glad to see you, my little snowflake.

Little me: Can I sit on your lap?

Jesus: Yes. I love you. You are so special. You are important to me.

Little me: Is Father Michael with you?

Jesus: Yes, he is.

Little me: He hurt me.

Jesus: I know. I was there. It hurt me, too.

Little me: It did?

Jesus: I love you so much. It hurt me to see you in pain like that. I hurt me when you got me mixed up with Father Michael. The whole thing hurt.

Little me: Hold me.

Jesus: I will. (Long quiet hug)

Jesus: Your stomach hurts.

Little me: Yes.

Jesus: You are angry at my Michael.

Little me: Yes.

Jesus: I love him, too.

Little me: Oh.

Jesus: When my Michael died, I showed him what he did to you.

Little me: Oh.

Jesus: He almost died from pain. You see, he loves you too. It was me who gave him love for you.

Little me: You did?

Jesus: Yes. Do you remember his love?

Little me: Yes.

Jesus: He didn't mean to harm you. He didn't think you would remember.

Little me: Oh.

Jesus: Is it OK to bring him here?

Little me: OK. Not too close.

Jesus: OK.

Jesus: Tell him.

Little me: Father Michael, when you raped me, I felt angry and confused. You split open my rectum. It hurt to poop. I felt so much pain and hurt.

Father Michael: I am so sorry. I would never have done it if I had any idea it would harm you.

Little me: It did! I hated it. I thought I would burst. I was so angry. I am angry now!

Father Michael: I ask your forgiveness. Please forgive me. I am so sorry. I would never, ever harm you. I would give my life to undo what I did to you. I have suffered so much knowing what I did to you. Please forgive me.

Little me: I want to forgive you.

Little me: Jesus, I need your help. (Another long quiet hug)

Little me: I forgive you, Father Michael, in the Name of Jesus. I forgive you for hurting me.

Little me: Jesus, I am sorry for all the ways I've hurt myself over this, especially my stomach and I ask you to forgive me, to help me to forgive and to heal my stomach and rectum.

Little me: I forgive Costanzo in the Name of Jesus.

Little me: I'm going to take a nap now. I love you, Jesus.

I laid down my pens and stumbled to my bed and lay down. I fell asleep immediately. When the lunch bell rang I swam up to consciousness. I splashed water on my face and brushed my teeth. I had to sit on the bed again for a few moments before I was ready to leave the room. By the time I got to the dining room the food was blessed and everyone else was seated. I took my turkey salad and green salad and sat down with my amigos.

I asked BA if she could come to my room at 2:30 before our walk. I said I wanted to share something to her. She readily agreed.

I returned to my room, quiet and still shaken. I reread the dialog, and then lay down again, musing over it, making patterns in the ceiling with my eyes.

BA's quiet knock at 2:30 startled me out of my musings. I let her in and offered her my desk chair. She sat with quiet, rapt attention, her eyes never leaving my face, while I sat on the bed and read the dialog to her. By the end of it we were both sobbing. She had fetched my box of Kleenex, grabbed a handful for herself and put the box beside me on the bed.

I wept for a while, soaking my Kleenex. I laughed-sobbed out loud, "I wonder if this monastery buys Kleenex by the semi-load?"

When my sobs quieted, I asked if we could walk. BA grabbed the Kleenex box and folded many Kleenex into small squares. She stuffed both pockets of her white skirt with them.

We set out, leaving through the glass exit door near my room. We went to stand under the cottonwood by the gift shop. It felt good to experience the rising and falling of the wind and the sound of it in the cottonwood, to connect with the greater world of nature.

We began our walk. BA was quiet, allowing me to talk. I mused at God's sense of humor bringing me here with a Father Michael as our guest master and a Michael as one of our amigos.

Anxiously I warbled back and forth between the amazing wisdom of the dialog and less important things. BA remained silent, watching me intently.

I remarked on the wisdom of both my "big self" and my "little self" and how both had come together to make the interchange with Jesus and me and my abuser possible.

BA let me go on, repeating myself, going back and forth, processing and reprocessing the dialog. Sometimes when I'd break down weeping, she'd just hold me. Sometimes she would cry, too. We used up all of her Kleenex and both of my pocket handkerchiefs.

We made circuit after circuit of the grounds until the Vespers bell sounded. BA put her fingertips lightly on my lower back and asked if I was ready to go in. She was perfectly OK with skipping the service.

I was nearly myself again and chose to go into the chapel with her. I cannot say that the Praise songs or psalms lifted me up much, but I was OK.

BA stuck tight beside me at dinner. Afterward she asked if I wanted to walk more or if I wanted to be alone.

I chose to go to my room until the evening class. I didn't feel I could read the dialog again just yet, so I lay on my bed and looked at the ceiling. I hung in the tension of what had happened.

BA had hung in the tension with me that afternoon, showing me God's love. Now I attempted to hang there with Jesus, as He had shown Himself to me in the dialog.

When the alarm chirped, I went down the hall to the class-room and took my seat against the window. I picked up my sewing and bent my head over it. Abbot David again. More on spirituality.

I continued to hang in the tension of the dialog.

My whole life has been about forgiveness. The Near Death Experience called me to forgiveness and compassion. The prayer service the first week here gave me freedom from unforgiveness for four weeks. For four weeks I had been "back up on the ceiling, like I'd been in my NDE, free of judgment, full of compassion.

Now I have to go back home and integrate what I have learned. I will have to endure more hurts from the people who often hurt me at home and I will have to seek the grace to forgive them "seven times seventy."

At first I had hoped that I was healed of unforgiveness forever. Now I saw that I'd been given a wonderful respite from unforgiveness, but that challenges to forgive would go on, probably for my whole life.

Suddenly, in real time, I heard the Abbot say "God will not take you out of the desert, but He will make the desert bloom." My head snapped up from my stitching. *Whoa! If I hang in the tension with the Lord, the desert will bloom!* I scribbled down his words.

The Abbot then said something that it would take me years to "get," "There is no virtue in suffering if no greater good comes from it." He dismissed us and I fairly ran to my room.

I got ready for bed and crawled into bed. I left the light on and looked at the ceiling, tracing patterns in the knotty pine, for a long time. Then I switched off the light and slept.

first light
the sunflower's wait
requited

TWENTY SEVEN

1995, Pecos Benedictine Monastery, Week IV, Friday

My eyes popped open a few moments before my alarm chirped. I lay in bed, enjoying birdsong, then sat up and pressed the alarm switch down.

I got ready and hurried down the hall. The grandfather clock sounded the hour just as I arrived. Michael was already waiting.

I pushed open the heavy wooden door carved with a descending dove and we stepped outside into the mountain cool air.

For the last time, we headed up the yellow-orange dirt driveway and through the stepped adobe pillars. We crossed the road and walked right a few hundred feet to the jeep trail.

We were much fitter than we'd been four weeks before, but the jagged rock that made up the trail still required careful placement of our feet.

On the way up, I asked Michael if, when he lived at Christ in the Desert, he had become attuned to when the bells would call him to chapel. He said that he did come to anticipate the bells. Rarely, when engrossed in his work, he would be surprised by the bell and have to hustle to bring closure to his task before chapel.

We climbed to the moaning pine, not at all breathless, and paused to look around us. The pine still had three strands of barbed wire in its heartwood, but my heart no longer had barbed wire in it. I was free of resentment at having to come back here after my Near Death Experience; I had forgiven the two people in my life that liked to "torture" me; I had spent four weeks free of the unforgiveness that had plagued me, four weeks "back on the ceiling of my Near Death Experience;" I had renewed my marriage commitment; I had forgiven Father Michael for what he had done to me and I had had a wonderful, safe, four weeks at a monastery crawling with priest spiritual directors.

I laid my hand gently on the trunk of the moaning pine and bid it goodbye. I strode down the mountain, a free woman with a heart filled with gratitude.

In my room, I kicked off my sneakers and slipped on my comfortable old Birks. I entered the chapel with a heart full of joy.

The Praise songs lifted me up even farther. I felt like my spirit was bumping against the sky-blue ceiling of the chapel.

My joy persisted through the Eucharist.

Breakfast was joyful. We were all looking forward to returning to our homes.

Our first class was with a short, curly haired nun. She spoke of "Presence of the Spiritual Director." Thérèse stressed the need to respond to the directee with immediacy and presence.

We must bring a vivid inner alertness that is at once calm and alert. Other virtues important in the Spiritual Director are compassion and integrity.

She said something that I had heard a few of my psychotherapy teachers say: you must be willing to risk that the process in Spiritual Direction will bring transformation to you as well as to the directee.

Mother Delores has told me that our work together has changed her. It certainly has changed me.

The nun cautioned us that the Spiritual Director's fatigue, busyness or excess of emotion can thwart the Spiritual Direction process.

After a break outside in the sun, we returned to the classroom to hear Brother Matt speak about Carmelite Spirituality.

This interested me greatly. Five years before, after a period where I had arisen at 4:45 a.m. to sit on the living room couch and pray for an hour, I had fallen into a strange state.

The state was reminiscent of the state I'd been in at age 19, when I'd lost my faith. As before, I no longer took any consolation in prayer or worship. I lost the ability to imagine. I lost the ability to be interested in much of anything.

My Spiritual Director, Mother Dolores, referred me to the book, *Dark Night of the Soul*, written in the 1400s by St. John of the Cross, a Carmelite priest. He described my condition to perfection.

It is a state where we are tested by God. A state where we are invited to reach out our hand into the darkness and step forward, trusting that God will grasp our hand.

The first time I was in the Dark Night of the Soul, in college, I had not known what it was and was not in a position to consult a Spiritual Director. Like many who fall into that Dark Night without the guidance of a Spiritual Director, I flunked it.

Now, with Delores' help, I had stepped out in the darkness in faith and successfully navigated this test.

I was rewarded with a return to faith, a faith that was strengthened and again perceptible. I had come to understand that this desolation was a gift from God, an "election," as St. John of the Cross described it, a testing to bring me closer to God.

I had basked in this new union with God for some time. Then the second darkness came: the Dark Night of the Spirit. Another howling darkness.

Where the first darkness had been marked by a deadening of the five senses and the inability to enjoy prayer or worship, the next was odder and much worse. I felt like everything that I sensed or felt or knew was "off." I renamed it the "Dark Night of the Stereo." I felt like I was the tall stack of stereo equipment in our family room; a stack on which someone had twisted every single knob askew.

The Dark Night of the Spirit, according to St. John of the Cross, purges us of any "ideas," "theology," "societal beliefs" or "fleshly self-centeredness" that interferes with our union with God while we are still here in the flesh.

Job, who was a righteous, upright, devout man who feared God, was stripped of his health, his family, his possessions and his old theology of "reward for good behavior." After resolving his Dark Night of the Spirit, Job entered into a new love affair with a cherished and loving God and "got his life back."

As I moved through this second darkness, I began to be "back on the ceiling" again, stripped of all theology and of all of my fleshly proclivities. Once again I had to step out in faith and trust that God would be there.

Like Job, the God I found was one of mercy and light, compassion and understanding. The vengeful-punishment God of my Catholic upbringing was gone.

I must admit that this Darkness returns from time to time. Apparently the process of purification was not complete and I need "tune-ups" every now and then.

Lunch was turkey spaghetti.

The four amigos spoke of how we longed to be at home with more variety in our protein sources.

We decided to go for a walk together after lunch. We returned to our rooms briefly and then met at the door to the guesthouse facing the river. I had put on my white shirt and hat.

We strolled the grounds talking of our time at the monastery together, our trips to Harry's and Renate's and our visits with each other.

On our second round, Daisy, the dog, walked with us as far as the river.

We had Small Group that afternoon.

We met in the Library. We gave updates on our prayer projects and stated our new prayer requests. We turned to our topic for the day, "Healing and Forgiveness in Spiritual Direction."

These are a few of the ideas that came up: Spiritual Direction bears witness to the directee's suffering; this makes the directee feel heard and feel valuable.

Spiritual Direction can heal fissures in the soul of the directee caused by abandonments, abuse and neglect if the Director is present and faithful.

The Director always puts the directee's needs first.

The non-judgmental love of the Director can lead to growth in the directee, with the directee becoming a more loving person.

The Director's compassionate listening may lead the directee to confess sin; to forgive hurts; to heal or to discern the directee's own next step on her journey with God.

Forgiveness of others and the self is part of the liberation process for the directee. Forgiveness is not something the Director pushes or advocates, but something that arises naturally as the directee experiences unconditional love from the Director.

After Small Group, I repaired to my room to pack and reflect. I read through my notebook and prepared the testimony I would give to my classmates and the Community that night after Compline.

At four I knocked softly on BA's door. She greeted me with a tight hug.

I was again white shirted and hatted; she wore one of her snow-white skirts. She had finally confessed that the way she kept her skirt so white was to have three of them. She wore each one of them only once and then laundered it.

We visited about our time together and vowed to stay in touch before we saw one another at the follow up two weeks next summer.

It was beastly hot so we made only one circuit of the grounds. We went into a sunny consultation room just off the classroom and sat in the orange plaid recliners visiting until the bell for Vespers.

We joined the amigos in the pew. The singing and psalms were uplifting.

Dinner was turkey Salisbury steak with those same mixed vegetables.

After dinner I called Sarah. Today was the last day that she and Robin had helped the teacher. Tomorrow they would pack for their trip to their Science Camp for Girls at Texas Women's University. They were both excited about it. She and I prayed for her back. "Whoa." she said, "I got really, really hot that time."

After dinner Abbot David taught us about Discernment, one of the gifts of the Holy Spirit. He reminded us that the Holy Spirit was the real Spiritual Director and that if we remained open to the leadings of the Spirit at every moment, we would not get in the way of the real Spiritual Director.

We had time for a short break and then the bell sounded for Compline.

After Compline we all repaired to the classroom where a lectern was set. Never one to lead the pack, I waited until near the end to stand and make my way to the podium.

I spoke of the first healing service and the infilling of forgiveness and, later, in the night, joy.

I thanked Abbot Andrew for not giving up on me that night. I spoke briefly of my Near Death Experience and of my sense that my life task was forgiveness. I expressed my gratitude for the four weeks of "being back on the ceiling" in a state of nonjudgmentalness and compassion. I hoped, I said, to make compassion more of my day-to-day life.

I told of the moaning pine and how, over the time of the four weeks, the strands of barbed wire that had grown into my heart had been cut, one by one. I expressed my prayer that if any of my listeners had barbed wire grown into their hearts that God would begin to remove it.

Afterword, introvert that I am, I hurried back to my room. I listened to Sarah's tape for me and put the two pictures she sent on the wall. I crawled into bed and fell asleep immediately.

the swallow returns
three mouths
open silently

TWENTY EIGHT

1995, Pecos Benedictine Monastery, Week IV, Saturday

My eyes opened before the alarm went off. I enjoyed snuggling in bed for a few moments and then arose. I got ready and made my way alone to the river door of the guesthouse. Michael was sleeping in.

I walked two circuits of the grounds alone, greeting the ducks and noting the swelling purple grapes on a fence near the duck pond. When I heard the bell calling the monks to chapel I headed back to the guesthouse and changed shoes.

I slipped into the tiny room off of the chapel and leaned into the wall, again placing my hands on either side of the chalice mosaic. I prayed for the Community all through their Eucharist. I could hear them singing at times and chanting psalms at times, but I could not make out any words.

When I heard them exit the chapel, I exited my little room and made my way to my "place in the sun," the seat where I normally sat during classes. Shortly I heard my classmates talking and laughing, approaching the classroom.

Breakfast was jovial. We were all excited about going back to our homes the next morning. I celebrated with a nunsuch banana.

Our first class was Abbot Andrew speaking about the use of Scripture in Spiritual Direction. He reiterated that the deeper our knowledge of Scripture was, the easier it would be for the real Spiritual Director, the Holy Spirit, to nudge us toward particular scriptures to help the directee.

He stressed that the Scriptures were inspired by the Holy Spirit and that the Holy Spirit stood ready to reveal the meaning of the Scriptures to us and to our directees.

After our break we had our last class of the session. The short curly-haired nun taught us again.

She spoke of re-entry to our lives after living on Planet Pecos for four weeks. She said that she hoped that none of us planned to go to work on Monday. Several people groaned.

Now you tell us! Fortunately, I had the week off. I had remembered how at the Glorieta Retreat last year tall Sr. Theresa had twitched when I spoke to her in my soft voice. I had planned to be home, quite alone, for the first week. Sarah would be at science camp and I would have time to adjust to "real life" with its chaos and clamor.

I went to my room after class to work on packing. I listened to Sarah's tape for the day and looked at the final two photos she'd sent.

I pulled all of the photos off of the wall and removed the teacher's putty that had held them. I rolled the putty into a gray ball and added it to the larger container of putty. I put all of the photos in a Ziploc bag.

I did my laundry and laid out my clothes for the journey home: khakis, orange tee, orange waist ribbon and orange socks. I laid a khaki sweater on top. I packed everything else but my blow dryer and my toiletries. My journal would go into my carry-on.

Soon it was time for lunch. Our last lunch of the session. Asian turkey salad and fresh baked biscuits. Tasty. We were alternately somber and jokey, a nice reflection of our mixed feelings about departure.

BA and I walked after lunch, jabbering away like the BBFs that we'd been since meeting. We sat by the waterfall for a long time, just talking.

We returned to the guesthouse just in time for our School Eucharist. Costanzo would be the celebrant. It was a quiet Mass punctuated with Praise songs.

Dinner was turkey meatloaf with "those" vegetables. We were rather somber at dinner.

I called Sarah. She was very excited about leaving for Science Camp for Girls in the morning. She would arrive at the dorm at Texas Women's University while I was still flying.

After Compline there was a "Celebration of Thanksgiving" with all of the School participants, all of the monks and oblates.

Tall Sister Theresa, the resident baker who was so good at making us cry, had outdone herself. Lavish quantities of warm chocolate chip cookies, the chips still melted, and homemade lemonade to wash them down with.

I saw quite a few tearful conversations and quite a few hugs. I mostly hung with my homies and slipped away early to my room.

I lay on my bed and traced patterns in the knotty pine ceiling with my eyes. What a wonderful four weeks it had been. I couldn't wait to get home and I couldn't wait to come back next year. Soon I was drowsy. I got up and switched off lights, crawled into bed and fell into a delicious sleep.

walking
the morning glory's spiral
an ant

TWENTY NINE

1995, Departure

My eyes opened and my heart gave a thump. Departure after breakfast! I got ready and finished packing. I had about a half an hour before Morning Praise and Eucharist and the ground was dry; I closed my suitcase and headed out the side door of the guesthouse to the dirt road.

I made one, slow clockwise circuit of the grounds, returning to the guesthouse just as the bell rang for chapel.

I was the last of the four amigos to arrive. I sat beside BA.

The Praise music was wonderful and the Eucharist was uplifting.

Breakfast was a happy cacophony of chatter. I had another nun-such banana with my cereal. Soon it was time to say goodbye to Coy, who was driving home.

BA, Michael and I would take the bus the monastery had hired to take us to the Albuquerque airport. The bus was waiting when we came down from breakfast.

I returned to my room for my watch, my huge rolling suitcase and my carry-on. I buckled on my fanny pack. I checked to make sure my paper ticket was in my carry-on pocket then rolled my suitcase down the hall.

Through the hall window, I saw Coy drive away. I knew he had a ten-hour drive ahead of him.

I exited through the door by the grandfather clock and rolled my suitcase up to the bus. The driver stowed it in the luggage area.

BA, Michael and I decided to board the bus early and take the very back row, where we could sit three across.

Soon the others boarded and we were away. Father Bernie, the School Director, waved goodbye.

I looked up as we passed the adobe pillars and saw the familiar sign on the left one *Via con Dios*: Go with God.

We three amigos chattered away and the time to Albuquerque passed in no time. Michael was headed to his new Mother House in central Texas, BA to Ohio and I to Dallas.

We arrived at the airport and disembarked. One last hug for each of the other two and I headed for American Airlines. I checked in, checked my bag and headed to the gate, boarding pass in hand.

I was a half hour early for boarding. Moving through the terminal and sitting at the gate, I was keenly aware of all of the noise and bustle of the airport. So unlike the monastery. I pulled out my red notebook and began to read.

The flight was called; I stowed my notebook for boarding.

I had a window seat again; I pulled my red notebook back out. Sparkles of red light danced across the airplane wall and the back of the seat in front of me. I continued to read. Soon we took off. The white noise of the plane nearly overwhelmed my Planet Pecos soul. I finished reading the notebook just as we landed. I put it away and disembarked.

Sarah's dad was there to meet me with a quick hug. The Dallas airport was busy and noisy. It took a lot of energy out of me to cope with it.

Sarah had left that morning for science camp with Robin. I had made special arrangements to visit her there in the afternoon. Sarah's dad drove me the 45 minutes to Denton, where Texas Women's University is located.

We were silent for the drive. I was grateful for the quiet. We made our way to where the girls were. I was exhausted before we got there.

Fortunately the girls had already bonded with the other campers and were not in the least bit interested in interacting with me beyond brief hugs and a quick chat about the plane ride. I was grateful to cut our visit short.

We'd have a long visit with Sarah the next Sunday and take her out for a meal.

I was glad to head for home. After another silent ride of 40 minutes we were at the house; I excused myself to take a nap. Wow, that nun was not kidding about re-entry.

I got up from my nap and made us a simple supper. Then we watched a quiet movie. Afterward, I tumbled into bed. The movie was so loud!

I got up early the next morning to walk my usual 5:30 a.m. predawn three miles. That was more like it. No cars, no noise, just the dark and at six, the dawn awakening the birds. I stood under "my" cottonwood and listened to its leaves crescendo and decrescendo in the dawn wind. I felt like I was home again.

Sarah's dad was gone when I got back. I walked through my house, touching everything, getting to know the house again. I went out into the garden, which was doing fine thanks to automatic sprinklers. The soft pink crepe myrtles were now in bloom behind the house. The pool sparkled in the sunlight.

I bathed and weighed myself. I'd lost 15 pounds. I didn't know if it was all of that walking or all of that turkey. Probably both.

I spent a quiet day. I put away my things and stowed my suitcase in the garage. I put my Bible, books and notebook on the dining room table so that they would be close at hand.

I took the quilt squares to my sewing room and unpacked them. I had finished 90 squares during the four weeks, the number I needed for Sarah's quilt. I had infused each square with prayer for her.

I'd done my laundry at the monastery and Sarah and her dad did their own laundry, so there was little for me to do. I sat and processed my time at the monastery. I'd been on Planet Pecos and now I was back in my life. Later when I went to the grocery store, I was again overwhelmed with the busyness, the sounds and all of the visual stimulation.

I saw Mother Delores on Thursday. We laughed about the turkey. She told me that she hadn't mentioned it to me ahead of time because I was such a healthy eater.

On Sunday we went to Denton to see Sarah for Parent's Day. She was delighted to see us. We went to a Greek restaurant and then visited a snow-cone stand close to the girl's dorm; they had walked over there several times during the previous week.

The next Friday night, we went back to Denton for the closing ceremony of the camp. Both girls got awards.

At the end the camp director stood and announced that the counselors had created a special award, one never given before. She asked Sarah and Robin to come forward. She gave them a special award for the campers who "sounded the most like an old married couple," BBFs since they were five, they were finishing each other's sentences and jumping into old arguments in the middle. The audience was convulsed.

After the ceremony we went to Sarah's room and picked up her things, then headed home. She fell asleep in the car on the way. So did I.

I kept my promise that Sarah could make ice cream. I gave her some cookbooks and turned her loose in the kitchen. She came up with grape ice cream. "It needed a little something, so I added rose water," said my little gourmet.

Gradually I got back into my life. Back to church. And meetings. And prayer groups. It all seemed so intense. I saw a few patients that second week back. Thankfully they were all clergy-people and rather sedate.

in the distance
blue rain
from a blue cloud

THIRTY

1996, Back to Planet Pecos

The year until the next session of the School was quite eventful.

A few days after Sarah returned from camp we learned that she had to have a fusion of eleven of her vertebrae. Surgery was scheduled for late September.

The doctor in the Scoliosis Clinic gave me "informed consent" for the surgery. Sarah could die; she could wake up paralyzed; she could wake up without bladder and bowel control. For several weeks I spent my 5:30 a.m. walks mud wrestling with God.

Can we still be friends if she dies? Can we still be friends if she wakes up from the surgery paralyzed below the waist? Can we still be friends if she loses bowel and bladder control?

I needed to come to grips with these questions. Ultimately I came to know, deep in my soul, that God and I could still be friends if any of these tragedies were to befall Sarah. This knowing allowed me to enter the difficult months ahead in peace.

An interesting thing happened the night before the surgery.

My friends from the prayer ministry and I were gathered around Sarah in the huge two-story atrium of Texas Scottish Rite Hospital for Children. We laid hands on her and were praying for Sarah and the surgery the next morning. A black man was near us buffing the bright orange linoleum; his back was to us.

When we finished praying he hurried over to us, tripping over his words in his excitement. "I am a Christian." "Are you Christians?" "I felt the waves of your prayers hitting my back." "It was powerful."

It was powerful. The surgery went very well.

I spent eight nights in the hospital with Sarah. After I brought her home, she was home from school for about three months, most of that flat on her back, including when she ate her meals.

Years later she would learn that "all" people with severe scoliosis had back pain before the surgery. Sarah never did have pain. We had prayed daily to avoid surgery; that prayer was not answered. But our prayers protected her from pain.

By the time she returned to school full time in January, the battle stripes on my left arm had faded completely.

Now it was the summer of 1996 and time to return to Planet Pecos. The two-week session began in mid-August.

I wanted to have access to a car so I planned to make the 11-hour drive to Pecos. I drove five hours the first day and met BA at a Holiday Inn in Amarillo; in the morning we drove the remaining six hours to the monastery in tandem.

I had a pad of pale yellow sticky notes on my dashboard and wrote 40 haiku on the drive to the monastery. I planned to put these haiku, and the ones I'd written the year before on the fixed pane of my room's window. People could vote for their favorites by placing shiny stars on them.

I had requested my old room, #19. When I got there I found a vase full of light magenta cosmos, a huge plate of freshly baked chocolate chip cookies and a lovely handwritten card with a quilt on the front. Sister Theresa had left these to welcome me back! Theresa and I had had quite a few quiet, deep chats the summer before.

I perused the syllabus. There were two unnerving changes. All of the nuns were now listed as Oblates, helpers. Most of these nuns had taken their perpetual vows as Benedictines and now they were Oblates!

Also, in the previous year, there had been a note in the syllabus expressing regret that ordained ministers from other traditions could not celebrate the Eucharist with the priests of Pecos. Last year the Pecos priests had expressed hope that this could change in the future. This sentiment was no longer in the syllabus.

Is this Planet Pecos or Planet Paradox?

I unpacked and went over to BA's room with the plate of cookies. We sat on the porch facing the river and ate them. Then we walked a circuit of the grounds.

The bell sounded for Vespers and we headed to the chapel. We saw Michael and Coy there and gave them both big hugs.

Turkey was still king at the monastery.

I had more quilt blocks with me for the second session but most of the teaching in the second session was new to me; I had little time to stitch.

We spent a lot of time studying the Enneagram, a personality typology that originated in Afghanistan 3000 years ago. The Jesuits learned of it and brought it out to the West. This material was all new to me so I had to write like crazy in the classes about the Enneagram.

The four of us got a new amigo that summer. Teal, who lives in north Texas, was back to finish her School. She had not been able to finish with her original class. She was a psychologist and a minister. She participated in a lot of our daytime amigo walks, in meals at the monastery and in our trips to dine at Harry's and Renate's.

During our two-week stay a single mother and her 19 year old Down syndrome daughter were staying at the monastery making a retreat. I was drawn to the daughter, Jill, as she reminded me so much of my brother Peter. I spent a lot of time with Jill and her mom.

I showed Jill how to make snapdragons snap. I gave Jill the small figurine of Pumba, the warthog from the Lion King, which I had brought with me to keep my prayer pig company.

My time with Jill stirred up powerful recollections of what was right with my family. We always went as slow as the slowest one. We always showed respect for babies by telling the baby if we were about to move the stroller or the shopping cart. We always announced, "Big Noise," if we were about to do something that would make a lot of noise.

I remembered how our family had stayed in our house in southeast DC after the NAACP "broke the block" and white flight ensued. We had to stay in DC until Peter secured a spot at the District of Columbia Training School.

There was no Special Education at that time and special-needs kids had to go to a state-run residential school. We gladly endured the many hardships of staying in DC in the suddenly mixed neighborhood.

Not all of the people who moved into the neighborhood were upstanding citizens. My sister and I endured quite a bit of bullying from groups of black youth who would take away our basketball or our bikes. We had our first exposure to unwed mothers; our new next-door neighbor had four daughters living with her; each had children born out of wedlock.

After Peter went away to school we moved to nearby Maryland.

As soon as we were allowed, we visited Peter every Sunday at the Training School in Laurel, Maryland. The school director told us that we were the only family who visited reliably.

Peter had a special friend at the school, Larry, a sweet-spirited black boy. We were permitted to take Larry with us on our outings on the grounds of the school. We would set up a picnic lunch on a picnic table by a large creek that ran through the property. We would eat, fish and play games like hide and seek.

The priest in our home parish had always refused to allow Peter to take communion. One Sunday Peter was home for the weekend. Peter stayed behind in the pew while the family went forward to take communion.

When we got back Peter was curled up in the pew sobbing his heart out. Dad took one look at him and said, "Come with me." When Peter stood up, Dad pulled out his handkerchief and dried his tears. Dad marched Peter up to the communion rail and showed him how to kneel down and how to hold his hands out. Dad stood behind him, arms crossed, stern eyes on the priest, daring the man to refuse Peter communion.

The priest gave Peter communion that day and any other time Peter was home to visit. It must have meant a lot to Dad to stand up to a priest and refuse to allow him to hurt his child.

During the second session at Pecos my amigo Michael did not want to hike in the mornings.

I tried hiking alone on the grounds the first morning I was there. It was still dark at 6 a.m. I took a nasty fall on the stone steps leading down from the river door of the monastery. After getting up, I used my flashlight to help me circle the grounds.

This is not going to work.

After that I walked indoors, making circuit after circuit in the J-shaped guesthouse, walking for 30 minutes until the bell for Morning Praise and Eucharist. This was much more like my prayer walks at home. I could wear my Birks, too. No rattle-snakes inside!

Jack was assigned to another small group. Costanzo was back at the Mother House in Siena, Italy. Ann and Dick were both back in the Small Group. We had a wonderful addition to our group, Mitch, an Episcopal priest from New Zealand; he had previously graduated from the School and was retaking the second session as a refresher course.

The group again agreed to be an intercessory prayer team for one another. We met a total of five times in the two weeks. We were tasked to discuss Spiritual Direction cases we had worked with. The group bonded quickly; our time together was fruitful, congenial and conflict free.

In the Enneagram typology, I had come out a "five." So did the priest from New Zealand.

We had an exercise where we were placed in a small group for one hour with people who were our same "number." I must confess that I had always secretly harbored the notion that if the world were filled with people just like me it would be a better place; this small group experience permanently disabused me of that notion.

We "fives" are observers. We like to sit back and watch and then, at the end, make a single pithy comment. I had to lead the group of six "fives" all of whom wanted to sit back and watch while composing their single pithy comment.

I am pretty sure that that was the worst hour of my life.

At first no one would talk. Mitch came to the rescue. He was the leader of a chaplaincy training program in his home city and he was a super "good sport." He knew two of the other "fives" and he made them talk. I bless him for that! Before he came to the rescue I was sweating and beginning to doubt my skills as a leader.

One of our classes was "Christodrama." I had skipped Compline and was already in the lower lounge looking out at the river. It began to rain. After Compline the monks led the rest of the class downstairs through the Cloister so they wouldn't have to get wet.

A priest, Father Bob, who had acted in Hollywood before joining the monastery, led the class.

He listed the characters in the gospel story of the healing of blind Bartimaeus and asked for volunteers to act out the drama. I am not drawn to acting, so I held back.

No one was willing to play role of Jesus so I volunteered. The class turned on me for a moment. "No one should want to play Jesus."

Aren't we all supposed to "play" Jesus? All the time? Isn't that the POINT of being Christian?

In the study for the Order of St. Luke the Physician, the healing ministry that I participated in, we study each of the twenty-six healing miracles of Jesus. We look at what He did and what He said. Twenty-six times.

For me, this study took me into the Heart, the Mind and the Spirit of Jesus. It caused me to trust the "red ink" in the Bible more than any black ink I found there.

I gladly took on the role of Jesus that day and healed blind Bartimaeus.

Last session I refused to say that my stick had burst into leaf, into new life. This year I stood up for what I believed no matter how much resistance I encountered from my peers. Growth!

We had several other memorable classes: "Self-Parenting the Inner Child;" "Aspects of the Healing Ministry;" "Obstacles and Hindrances to Spiritual Direction" and "Everything You Always Wanted to Know about Spiritual Direction but Were Afraid to Ask."

The last shone light on a remarkable fact: you can do Spiritual Direction anywhere, in an elevator, at the store. It does not have to be a scheduled thing. It can happen anywhere, anytime, with friends, with strangers.

My Spiritual Director for the second session was Father Paul. Because he bore such a striking resemblance to my abuser I had been "sure" that I would be assigned to him in the second session. I figured it would be like the "Michael thing" in the previous session.

I had always felt that Paul and I were in a mind meld whenever he was teaching or preaching; the few times we had exchanged words our communication had been telegraphic. In Spiritual Direction I found we did, in fact, connect at a deep level. We spoke often of the Healing Ministry, something that was important to both of us.

On the Sunday in the middle of the two-week session, BA and I drove to Santa Fe. We parked at the Inn at Loreto and walked toward the square.

There was a distinct buzz of virtue in the air. As we approached the square we saw dozens upon dozens of canvas tents. It was the Indian Market!

I had heard of the Indian Market. I had no idea that it would be this weekend and frankly, I had no idea that ALL Native American artists would be here.

Introvert that I am, I hung back listening at the artist's tables. I saw every single artist who had made the "storytellers" that I had collected. I heard each one of them speak of their devotion to Christianity. There was a lightness to the virtue that surrounded these artists.

A few of the other artists were dark and unsettling.

I bought a beautiful concho belt from a sweet Indian couple. I had looked for one with a yellow metal for years; most are silver. I got a brass one with inset carnelians. I am still in love with it after all these years.

The two weeks and thirty hours of instruction flew by. Soon it was time for witnessing.

I spoke of Jill, the young woman with Down syndrome, and my recovery of the knowledge that my dysfunctional family still had many wonderful things going for it.

I had turned in my book reports so I was eligible to be commissioned as a Spiritual Director; the few classmates who had not yet turned in their reports received "fake" diplomas. After the ceremony we had a festive dinner with PORK!

After Compline was a talent show. I read some of my haiku.

Then we had another celebration, a social with fresh lemonade and Theresa's still-warm chocolate chip cookies.

At the social, the four amigos from Texas and Oklahoma — Coy, Michael, Teal and I — agreed that we should have a reunion group once every month or two. We who had inhabited Planet Pecos for six weeks were now very different from our church friends. We wanted to continue to meet and to support one another's growth. Teal volunteered to organize the group. BA, who lives in Ohio, would not be able to join us.

The final morning I walked in the guesthouse, attended Praise and Eucharist, and ate breakfast with my amigos. Time for Departure.

An owl hooted as I put my suitcase in the trunk.

I made the 11-hour drive home in one day, stopping only for lunch in a tiny town. I had handmade chicken-fried chicken to restore my cholesterol. I wrote 37 haiku during the drive home. I made it home shortly after dark. I was glad to see my Sarah; she was better than any haiku moment.

two weeks passed
three new grasses
in bloom

THIRTY ONE

Reunion, 1996-2001

Teal was true to her word. She organized a reunion group six weeks after our graduation. Teal, Coy, Michael and I planned to meet for lunch at a hotel near Dallas Fort Worth airport.

Unbeknownst to Teal, the hotel had changed its name. Coy, Teal and I figured it out and met in front of the hotel. We hadn't seen Michael yet so we walked down a slight hill to the corner to watch for him. Seconds later Michael drove up. We waved wildly and pointed him to the parking garage. We trooped back up the hill and waited for him by the fountain in front of the hotel.

We were delighted to see one another. Over lunch we shared how strange the "real world" seemed after Planet Pecos. Michael was able to help us with our transition since he had lived at a monastery for seventeen years and then had to transition back to "real life." It took him a whole year.

Teal and I were settled back into our therapy practices. Michael had been named Formation Director for his order at their Mother House in central Texas. Coy was back at work in his ministry with the Disciples of Christ.

We met for lunch five times at the hotel near the airport, then I suggested meeting at my home. The others were enthusiastic. We could speak in privacy and sit on couches or on the floor as we visited.

I began cooking special dishes for these meetings. Once I made my honey whole wheat bread and served it with a tasting menu of seven types of butter from the US and Europe. Another time I made my flourless chocolate cake that has "pharmacological" amounts of chocolate in it. I served it with a big bowl of whipped cream.

Sarah and Robin and I took a day-trip to the Mother House to visit Michael. The church on the grounds of the Mother Mouse was one of Texas' famous "painted churches." It had stunning murals on the walls and ceiling, all in Southwest tones.

In 1997 Michael was transferred to a parish in San Marcos, Texas. Teal and I drove down for his ordination as a transitional deacon. He was finally on his way to being priested.

Teal and I got to San Marcos early and visited the spot where the San Marcos River bubbles up from the ground over a span of about 20 yards. On the path back to our car we met an enormous swan. Her leg had a huge aluminum band on it with a serial number. She would peck at it and then look at us beseechingly as if asking us to remove it.

We got to Michael's church, St. John's, early and planted moonflower seeds along the chain link fence of the playground to commemorate his ordination.

We met Michael in the sanctuary at four. He had asked us to pray for a little girl with leukemia. We laid hands on her, asking for complete healing. (Months later he let us know that lab tests showed no sign of the leukemia.)

Teal and I sat in a front pew and visited until the church filled for the 5 p.m. service of ordination. The service was beautiful. There was a mariachi choir. Several of the women sang while swaying and holding their children on their hips. Bishop Placido Rodriguez officiated.

At one point in the service Michael knelt in front of him and the Bishop took Michael's folded hands in his own with great tenderness. He asked Michael to promise obedience to his Superiors.

We sang the song that Michael had chosen at Pecos for his ordination, *The Servant Song*.

The reception was quite wonderful. The parishioners had made their best Mexican dishes. The mariachi band had moved over to the parish hall and continued to sing. To our delight, the Bishop was a mariachi singer and joined the band, donning a huge circular hat with golden dangles.

The reunion group continued to meet at my house every month or two until Michael was transferred to a parish in Orange County, California.

At that point Coy suggested that Teal and I meet him halfway between Dallas and his home in Oklahoma. Lake Murray, Coy told us, is a mature manmade lake; all of the rough edges have been smoothed out over the decades and it looked like a natural lake.

Coy had told us that we would be in fried-pie country. He suggested that we take turns bringing the fried pies. He would get them just off I-35 at exit 51 in Oklahoma. We could get them in Gainesville, Texas on the town square. I agreed to bring the fried pies to our first meeting at Lake Murray.

I picked up Teal at a shopping center at the intersection of I-35 and Highway 121. We drove north on I-35 until we reached Gainesville. I turned east towards the town square. At the square I turned right again and parked on the far corner.

We could smell the pies when we got out of my car. The smell of hot fat is a wonderful smell if you are about to consume a fried pie.

As we left the car we noted that there was a Mobile ICU and an ambulance parked in front of the Fried Pie Company. *Maybe a patron has collapsed from the cholesterol!* Closer inspection showed that both vehicles were turned off and empty. Their crews were inside eating fried pies!

We bought three coconut and three cherry fried pies. The counter girl wrote the flavor of each on a piece of white bakery paper; she wrapped each of the pies in a labeled sheet and placed the six pies in a white bakery box.

On our way out we walked around the edges of the restaurant perusing the items against the wall, which were for sale. There were Christmas trees made of pine cones and strand after strand of Christmas lights in the size and shape of shotgun shells; cylinders with brass bottoms.

We returned to the car and opened the white box. The pies had been made from eight-inch circles of dough. The filling was added and the dough was folded into a half circle; then the edges were crimped tightly before frying. The final size of the pie was six inches along the straight edge.

I selected a coconut pie. The pie was still warm from the fryer and was heavy in my hand. The filling was loaded with shreds of coconut. It was divine. Teal selected cherry and dug in. We polished them off in no time.

We returned to I-35 and set out for Lake Murray. We turned off at the exit for the lake. The crest of the first slow hill had been cut into by the road builders; 15-foot walls of sedimentary rock rose beside the road on both sides. There were two more slow hills and then we could see the park ahead.

We stopped at a gas station/convenience store to use the restroom. As we creaked our old bones out of the car we saw Coy creaking out of his car. We laughed at ourselves, used the facilities and followed Coy's car to the lodge.

We had hot chocolate at the café overlooking the lake.

We visited the front desk for a map of hiking trails and sat in rockers in front of a huge fireplace, its stones blackened with age. While studying the map we put our feet up on bolsters in front of the fire. The fire screen was made of wrought iron and portrayed deer leaping.

We chose the trail to the "Point" jutting out into the lake. I begged Coy and Teal for a moment to look at the huge fish tank to the right of the fireplace; it was stocked with fish native to Oklahoma.

Outside, I grabbed the pie box out of my car and we piled into Coy's car to drive to the trailhead.

We parked by rustic cabins and stepped carefully down a short but steep hill, then walked across a flat, grassy meadow. We entered the woods. We crossed a small bridge over a creek and hiked the mile to the point. The walk was exhilarating. It felt so good to hike with friends from Planet Pecos.

We sat at the picnic table on the point and ate pie. This time I had one filled with tart cherries. It still bore a trace of warmth from the fryer.

There was one coconut pie left. Coy laid the last pie on its white paper on the picnic table, pulled out his pocketknife and cut it into three pieces. We were glad that we'd remembered to bring napkins.

When we were done, we rinsed our hands in the lake and returned to the picnic bench.

We sat and talked for an hour and a half then meandered back to the car.

Coy suggested a catfish restaurant on the left on the way back to I-35. He dropped us at my car and we followed him to the restaurant. Crunching onto the gravel and dirt parking lot brought back memories of driving into Harry's.

Fried catfish with hushpuppies is one of the most divine meals imaginable, especially for turkey-traumatized people. The day was mild so we ate out on the deck. The deck stretched out over the steep hill; we were 15 feet above ground level, looking straight into the forest.

We continued to meet monthly or bimonthly, listening to one another, supporting one another and eating fried pies and catfish. Coy would bring the pies one time and we'd bring them the next.

Teal and Coy supported me as I wrote my book *Rx for Quilters.*

A very strange thing happened in 2000 during one of our reunion visits. I was very seriously considering divorcing my husband. As we walked the trail to the point I shared my dilemma with Coy and Teal. I was feeling like I was suffering with little "greater good" except being available 24/7 to Sarah. They listened, only speaking to ask me questions.

On the way back to the car, we crossed a low sandy area. Scratched in the sand with a stick were the words "don't go." We all kept a straight face, as our separate professions had trained us to. There did not seem to be a single other person on the point with us.

Who wrote that? That's just what Sarah said to me when I was waiting to board my flight to New Mexico in 1995. I had gone and it had been fine.

Over lunch I finally shared how much the words in the sandy soil had freaked me out. Coy and Teal listened intently, respectfully but offered no advice.

We met twice more after that. It seemed like we were finally re-integrated into our "real lives" again.

Occasionally Coy would be in Dallas on church business and I'd meet him for lunch at Cheddar's on Highway 75 as he headed back to Oklahoma.

Teal and I met for lunch occasionally, sometimes in Grapevine and sometimes in Dallas. Her friendship would become very valuable to me after I decided to divorce.

In 1998, I travelled to Ohio to give a Mother's Day Retreat, "The Authority of a Mother's Prayer," at BA's parish. It was wonderful to see her after a diet of phone calls and letters.

In 2000 I was in Los Angeles to tape anHGTV show about the book I had written, *Rx for Quilter:,Stitcher Friendly Advice for Every Body.* I drove to Michael's church in Orange County to see him celebrate Mass.

Afterward he borrowed the pastor's car and took me to the Mission that was his order's west coast base. We walked through gardens bright with blossoms. He showed me the church and sacristy.

Outside again, we visited the Order's graveyard. "This is where I will be buried," he said quietly. *How wonderful to know exactly where you will be.*

don't go
don't go
don't go

THIRTY TWO

Coming Home

In 2001, ten days after Sarah left for college, I filed for divorce. Twelve days later was 9/11. I made a strategic decision not to "do" 9/11; the changes in my life being quite enough to occupy me.

I set up an office of my own.

One day, the day of the winter solstice, I was driving up the road that my office is on, heading to my lawyer's house. I heard a very loud voice say, "Turn on the next street."

Just for the record, psychiatrists HATE hearing voices and I almost never hear this voice. I was eager to get to my attorney's so I said, "I am NOT in the mood." But I turned onto the street.

I had lived on that street 15 years before. We had rented a house on that street for our first year in Texas. As I cruised along the street I saw a "for sale" sign on the north side of the street. I pulled over. The voice said, "This is the house." I said, "I TOLD you, I am not in the mood." But I copied down the information.

I have to admit the house looks beautiful in this lemon light of the solstice.

When I finished with my lawyer, I called the number and listened to the recorded announcement. I called and made an appointment to view the house. I was pretty sure I had lived next door.

The house for sale had been a rental house since it had been built. It had now been sold to a rehabber. It had the same floor plan as the house I'd rented. I had loved that house. I told the rehabber that I'd lived next door 15 years before. "This house has the same floor plan as the one I rented." I told him I would call him. I was very interested.

When I got home I looked at stationery I still had from when I lived on that street. It was the same house! I had been thrown off by the lack of a 25-foot willow on the left side of the yard, the presence of a 30-foot sycamore on the right side, and the new reddish roof.

Legally I could not make an offer on the house until the divorce was final. The rehabber knew that I had the money to buy it and thankfully he waited for me. In the meanwhile he made some repairs that the inspector had turned up.

On the day of the divorce I went to the county courthouse for the "prove up" of the agreement the two lawyers had hammered out.

A few hours later I went to meet my ex at a gift shop *cum* notary where I had always gone to get Sarah's school papers notarized. Sarah called just as her dad pulled up. I waved him over to the car to speak with her. Then we went inside.

"Can you notarize some papers for us?" "I saw you two sitting in the car together. Is this a lover's tryst?" "No," I said," "Agreement Incident to a Divorce." The poor man, a retired engineer, choked.

I came home to my old house in mid-February, ten days after the divorce was final. The mover took two trips to bring my stuff over. As luck would have it, I was giving a talk about my book to a quilt guild in Denton, Texas that night. I had signed the contract months before.

My dear friend JoAnn and her husband stayed at the house to receive the second load of furniture and to set up my bed for me and put the linens on it. When I came home exhausted, long after dark, it was wonderful to be able to fall into my bed.

Now it was eight months later, the Wednesday before Thanksgiving. I had been divorced and celibate for eight months. I had been kicking around the idea of returning to the Catholic Church.

I called my friend Vickie to discuss it.

Vickie and I had gone to an Episcopal church together years before. She had decided to return to the Catholic Church after much prayer and fasting. She had been back in the Church for several years by this time. She attended a church in a city not far from my own.

Vickie made one phone call and called me right back. A nun at her church, an administrator, said to come right over. She was sure that Father would be available very soon.

Wow, this is moving fast, I thought as I drove to the church, one new to me. The nun greeted me warmly. "Welcome home," she said.

Quietly, without my asking a thing, she fed me the canon law that I would need to get an annulment of the marriage. We chatted for a while about our lives. Then Father was available.

He took me back to his office.

He sat behind his huge desk. That was fine with me. I had no desire to get physically close to any Catholic priest.

"Please help me to understand the purpose of this confession," I said.

"The purpose is for you to unburden yourself of any sins that trouble you," Father said.

"I have had a confessor, an Episcopal Priest, for ten years. There is no sin that troubles me."

"Who was your confessor?"

"Mother Delores," I replied.

"Well, there is a question as to whether confessions heard by a woman are valid," he said.

"Well, Father, those confessions healed me, and that is all the validation I require."

He harrumphed a few times

He said, "Well, you must confess the sin of leaving the Catholic Church."

"Well, Father, a Catholic priest committed a crime against me when I was five years old. Ultimately that led to my leaving the Church."

He looked away, harrumphing a few more times. "Well, in certain circumstances, we make an exception."

That's really good of you, you asshole.

He jumped up. "I have to get something."

He came back with a book, his finger stuck in one page.

"Read this," he commanded, with no explanation.

I crossed my fingers and read it aloud. It was something to the effect that I was really wrong to leave the Church.

I uncrossed my fingers and Father gave me absolution.

"Where are you going to worship?" I knew he was hoping I would pick another parish.

"I have chosen St. X's, because the people there seemed to really want to come to church and worship. "

"Huh?" he said.

"Never mind."

At the other parishes in my town, people seemed to have one foot in the aisle near the end of the service, ready to bolt. At St. X's it was different.

He shook my hand and I left, shaking my head.

That was fun.

I set about going to church and getting involved in activities. I was still nervous and very aware of the need to keep myself safe.

One day I was walking at the mall with a woman from the Singles Ministry. She had a 12-year-old son. One of the priests in the parish had called her home and left the boy a message wishing him a happy birthday, suggesting that he cut school on the day of his birthday. I stopped breathing. *He's grooming him.* I was speechless. Really speechless. The truth is I did not have the words to say, "He might be grooming you, he might be grooming your son. Watch out!"

Oh no, oh no. Can I really do this, can I be a Catholic?

Typically priest-criminals groom the parents of the children first, and then move in on the kids. It is considered a great honor to receive attention from a priest. Here was a situation ripe for abuse of this child. The mom was pleased with the attention. The boy was pleased with the attention. I wish I had known how to speak to her.

Even today, now that I have the ability to speak up, I am not sure she would have listened to me. And, of course, there is no way, then or now, for me to know the intentions of the priest.

I joined the Catholic Physician's Guild. It was fantastic to be in a group with warm, virtuous Catholic physicians. The next rumbling that being Catholic was not going to work out for me came after I volunteered to write a three-sentence announcement about the upcoming physician/spouses retreat. This brief summary would be placed in all of the parish bulletins.

The priest that coordinated the Guild gave me the one page-flyer about the retreat from the previous year. "Write the three-sentence summary and run it by me before you send it to the deacon."

Seriously? You have given me last year's flyer with complete details and you want me to RUN THE THREE-SENTENCE SUMMARY BY YOU???? I guess there are no grownups in the Catholic Church. For goodness sake, the head deacon will be reading it before it goes out!

I was deeply insulted. After a few days I decided not to play. I emailed the priest and told him that I did not have time to write the three sentences.

The last straw came a month later. It was the annual ethics dinner for the Catholic Physician's Guild. It was held at a large Catholic hospital in Dallas. I came in a bit late and spied a table full of the physicians who regularly attended the Guild meetings. I sank into an empty chair.

The lecture began moments later. I turned my chair to face the speaker, a wonderful Jesuit ethicist from Georgetown University. After the lecture I turned back around and looked down at my plate.

The program lying on my plate told me that I was at the "Bishop Graumann Sanctity of Life Dinner." I couldn't breathe. Bishop Graumann had been found responsible in a court of law for transferring a known pedophile from parish to parish to parish.

I was done. I stood up quietly and with dignity walked out of the dinner and out of the Catholic Church.

I attended an Episcopal church for a few years after that. It was a great parish, but the worship was very high church; after Pecos I needed joyful worship.

I tried another mainline Protestant church for several years. The worship was great. I sang in the choir. I taught in the Sunday school classes that I attended. I was on the roster of Sunday school teachers with special topics and visited many Sunday school classes as a one-time teacher. But that church just wasn't right for me. I still maintain warm, valuable relationships with four women from that church.

Now I am at another mainline Protestant church. I love the joyful worship. I am a joyful participant in worship, in Christian Quilters and the prayer ministry. Next spring I will teach a class about the healing miracles of Jesus.

Thankfully, like Job, I am in a vibrant relationship with God. I seek joyful worship experiences but do not require them to stay connected to "God, who is my home." If for any reason this church does not work out, I will be OK.

dark earth
against light
ground squirrel's new burrow

THIRTY THREE

Planet Homeless

In early 2002, I found that I needed a bit more income. A recruiter called looking for a psychiatrist to work four hours a week at a clinic in Dallas. I filled out 56 pages of paperwork and faxed it to him.

The next day a woman from the clinic, Hope, called, "Would you consider working with the homeless?" *I cringed inwardly, thinking, I don't think so!* Since I had not had a job interview in decades I agreed to the interview "for practice."

Twenty minutes later an indescribable peace descended over my whole body. *This is the job!*

I remembered what Mother Teresa said, "You don't have to come to Calcutta. There are people in your town who need you. Find them and love them!" I knew right then that I would take the job if they offered it to me. I would put the lessons I'd learned at Pecos to the test.

I consulted a nurse friend about how to dress for the interview. "Dress down," she said, laughing uproariously.

Two days later I headed into downtown Dallas, 19 miles from my suburban home, dressed down. The Day Resource Center for the Homeless (DRC) was a block south of City Hall, with a large parking lot in between the two.

I drove around the parking lot and noted that the gate in the chain link near the DRC was locked. I found a numbered parking place on the City Hall side of the parking lot and visited the pay station, pushing a folded dollar bill into the slot corresponding to my parking space. I set off.

As I rounded the corner of the chain link fence I noticed a xeriscaped bed with prickly pear cactus just beginning to bud. *OK, God, I get the hint. There's going to be thorns, but I will blossom here.*

I walked down St. Paul Street toward the Day Resource Center and studied the building. It was an old red brick building. The second story had windows that opened outward; each with many small panes. Over the years broken panes had been replaced with whatever glass was available. The windows were now a mosaic of clear glass in several shades of pale green and pale blue. The replacement panes were also in several textures; a few panes were mirrored.

I crossed Cadiz Street with the light and saw that the near east end of the building had modern windows and a door. I approached the door and found it locked. I saw a nurse inside and signaled to her to open the door. She turned her back on me.

I saw people milling around the west end of the building. *Maybe the entrance is up there.* I headed that way. I passed an older woman dressed in ill-fitting filthy rags sitting on the sidewalk. She was having an angry conversation with an invisible person.

Further along the sidewalk was a tall box stuffed with clothing. I saw a homeless woman select a blouse from the box and then throw the hanger on the ground. My initial reaction was horror at the "littering." Later I would understand that when a person is sleeping on the sidewalk and has no idea of where her next meal is coming from, the concept of "litter" is not meaningful to her.

As I passed the huge storefront-like windows of the west end of the Day Resource Center, I noted a number of white Formica cubicles inside. They spanned the length of the windows. As I approached the small crowd of homeless men gathered on the sidewalk, I noted a wrought iron gate and fence around a small parking lot.

I navigated between groups of men and stepped onto the cement parking lot. The surface was filled with deep gouges and these were filled with dark liquid. A police officer spotted me and said, "Don't step in the puddles." I heeded his advice and maneuvered around them. A homeless man opened the first glass door for me, bowing at the waist. I pulled open the second glass door myself. The handle was unpleasantly greasy.

Straight ahead as I entered was a checkroom. The large bins were filled with black garbage bags each filled half full. I would learn that the homeless carry everything they own in these bags and that their belongings would be stolen every three weeks, on the average.

I turned left into the building and saw a hip-high white Formica rectangle. Inside were four police officers. I told them who I was and they waved me around to the left of their cubicle, sparing me a walk through the metal detector.

To my left, toward the windows, I could see the fronts of the Formica cubicles I'd seen from the street. Each was dedicated to social services of some sort, housing, food stamps and the like. Three rows of blue, stackable chairs stood facing the cubicles. The chairs were filled with slumped-over homeless persons in ill-fitting clothes.

I headed straight toward the hallway I saw ahead of me. As I moved out of the open area into the hallway I noticed that the walls were painted a sickly yellow. In the hall were two huge tables with clothing jumbled on them. Homeless women in various stages of disarray stood over the tables looking for clothing that might fit them.

As I proceeded down the hall I saw women sitting against the wall, many sleeping. I would learn that the homeless are afraid to go to sleep on the streets, needing to stay awake so that they could protect themselves. This was especially true of the women, who feared beatings and rape. The men mostly feared beatings, though they were raped by other men occasionally.

I continued down the hall and came out into another open area. I saw that I was in a medical clinic run by Dallas County, the Parkland Medical Clinic. Ahead, tucked in a corner, I saw a small office for the VA; a sign on the door gave the days and hours that it was open. In the back of the building were shower and laundry facilities.

I asked a nurse where the agency I was interviewing with was located and was directed back the way I had come.

Halfway down the corridor a man approached me. He was in his early 20s, sunburned and had a two-day growth of beard. He said, "This is my first day here, do you know where the restrooms are?" I replied, "It is my first day here, too, and I have no idea." I referred him to the police officers by the door.

When I got to the first hallway on my left, I turned and made my way down the hall. I poked my head into the first room I came to. It held four desks. Four heads looked up. I asked for Hope and received four smiles.

"You must be Dr. Delaney," said a slender black woman wrapped in humble dignity. I would later learn that she was Kathy. "Hope is waiting for you across the hall." She showed me to Hope's office and left me there.

Hope was a blond, blue-eyed woman dressed in jeans and a tee shirt. "We are excited to meet you. The team wanted to have input on who was hired this time," she said. "Let's go back to Kathy's office and we will have the interview there."

We crossed the hall again. Homeless Services workers quickly filled the large office. There was the woman responsible for financial assessments and medical records; the Homeless Services nurse; the addiction specialist and all of the caseworkers. The agency had seven offices in the building, three on this hallway and four on the hallway closer to the entrance to the building.

The team grilled me for half an hour about my experience with psychiatric patients, especially low-income people with very disturbed family systems. They began to describe some of the problems that their patients faced. Clearly they wanted to know if I had the mental toughness needed to work with their clientele. Fortunately I had had the training and experience to deal with them. Slowly smiles appeared on their faces. They were satisfied with my abilities.

Hope took me back to her office and offered me the job. I was to do a Thursday afternoon clinic for two weeks, then add a Thursday night clinic at a shelter run by the Episcopal Church, Austin Street Centre. I accepted. I told her that I wanted to shadow the other homeless psychiatrist before I began work.

We agreed that I would meet the team at the Stewpot, a homeless services center run by the Presbyterian Church, on the following Wednesday morning. I'd observe the clinic there and then follow the team to its Wednesday afternoon venue at Turtle Creek Manor, a drug treatment facility run by Dallas County.

The supervisor from the central office of the agency appeared. Hope left and he sat down with me. He explained the dangers of working with this population. Twenty percent of our patients had murdered; many were convicted of aggravated assault; others were rapists and pedophiles; some were prostitutes and others, burglars.

He openly expressed his dismay that the team had chosen a woman. He preferred to have men on the team who could do "takedowns" of unruly patients. I looked him in the eye and told him I would never participate in a takedown. I reminded him that four uniformed policemen and women were on duty 40 feet away.

I resolved in that moment to "bribe" the police gently by bringing a bag of Hershey's milk chocolate kisses every shift that I worked and giving it to them as I came in. It would be a benign bribe so that they would always "have my back."

On the next Wednesday morning I drove to the Stewpot, three blocks from the Day Resource Center. I greeted the guard as I drove into the multilevel garage. I parked and made my way to the first floor.

Seeing more puddles, I navigated around them and smiled at the guard again. He tipped his hat. I entered through the gray steel door and made my way along the hallway. The walls were lined with stunning photographic portraits of Dallas' homeless. I blinked back tears.

Farther along the hallway I found the conference room where the team was already setting up their computers and other equipment. Kathy walked me around the corner to the dental office, where the other doctor was already getting set up. The doctor greeted me warmly.

We sat on folding chairs backed tightly against the cupboards in the tiny dental office. A single TV tray served as our writing surface. A standard-sized dental chair filled most of the room. Its footrest intruded into the space we claimed for our interactions with patients.

Sitting there, waiting for our team to be ready, I could see the main desk of the Stewpot. At the elevated counter I saw a worker handing out multivitamins to homeless persons who requested them. I guessed that the worker had a quart bottle of vitamins!

I could see a paramedic doing blood pressure checks at a table to our right. Whenever he had an opening he'd go to the loudspeaker and announce free blood pressure checks. He never lacked for customers. Later I'd realize that health care workers were probably the only people in the city who would look the homeless in the eye, much less touch them.

We began our clinic. All of the patients were returnees. The doctor was kind to all. She was firm with those who had gone off their meds and with those who needed a bigger dose because they were too manic. Mania usually manifested as anger in the homeless. We saw 15 patients, all told, that morning.

As lunch approached, more homeless crowded the large central room that we could see from the dental clinic. Lunch would be served shortly. A Presbyterian minister came over the intercom to bless the food. The men shuffled through the line to get their plates.

We had three patients still waiting for us so our staff went over and got three foil-covered plates of food so they wouldn't miss their lunch.

When clinic was over the other doctor and I stood and stretched. The quarters had been very cramped and both she and I were stiff. Our support staff quickly broke down the clinic and packed it into the trunks of their cars. I was in awe of the flexibility and heroism they displayed in being willing to set up clinic *de novo*.

We caravanned to an Indian Restaurant where we enjoyed a delicious buffet. Indian food is probably my favorite "foreign" food.

Then we made our way to Turtle Creek Manor, the residential drug treatment center. The team carted the equipment up several floors and again set up in a conference room. The doctor and I got to sit in a spacious office with glass walls and a huge desk, a far cry from our cramped morning venue. We saw another 15 people, filling out the paper forms for office visits.

I thanked the doctor for allowing me to shadow her. She wished me luck with the new job. I bade the team goodbye and promised to be at the DRC the next day at noon.

The drive home was very pleasant. Turtle Creek Manor was close to Hillcrest Road, a lovely residential road that winds north from Dallas to distant suburbs.

I could see the fruit trees budding. A few brave plum trees were already in bloom, their pale pink flowers making a lovely contrast to their bare mahogany branches. *Thank you God, for these new buds in nature and in me. Be with me as I grow and blossom.*

The next day I headed downtown. I had lunch at the Nasher Sculpture Garden, sitting on the patio in the warm sun near a splashing fountain. I strolled through the garden visiting my favorite Henry Moore statue and the ponds beside it. Leaving, I put my phone in the pocket of my suit and my purse in the trunk of my car. "Don't tempt the mortals."

I drove the eight blocks between the upscale art museum and Planet Homeless. I was glad that I had "stoked up" on goodness before my shift.

I now had a key for the gate lock on my lanyard, so I could park near the center. I sat in my car for a few minutes and looked at the Day Resource Center. The west end of the building was faced with cobalt blue tiles. At one time the words Day Resource Center had been mounted on the tiles. Now only about half of the letters were in place. Many hung crookedly on their mounts.

I used my key to open the gate and then relocked it. I crossed Cadiz midblock and entered the DRC. I presented the police with their bag of Hershey kisses. Their grins stretched all the way back to their ears. Hope's desk was covered with a four-inch layer of papers and I had to push some of them back to make room for my work.

Kathy was going to help me flow the clinic. I asked her to come in and close the door. "Kat, What faith tradition do you follow," I asked. "Baptist," she replied. "Would you pray with me before we start the clinic?" Her answer was a huge smile.

She sat in the "patient chair." I began by reading Psalm 91, the prayer of protection that I'd learned about at the monastery. Then I asked God to show us the face of Jesus in the faces of each of the patients we would see that day. I asked Kat if she wanted to add anything, but she did not. I looked up. She was fanning herself and grinning. "I felt so hot when you started to read that psalm."

I saw about ten homeless, mentally ill men that afternoon, and had my heart broken ten times. Kat sat with me all afternoon, something that she would do for a few months, until I had my bearings.

I learned that the homeless were sometimes people like you or me who have been permanently sidelined by focal strokes, car accidents or on-the-job injuries.

Others were people with a good work ethic who were trapped in low-wage, no-benefit jobs. Nationwide, I learned, 15% of homeless shelter residents work five days a week.

Some homeless persons are veterans of US military service; often victims of Post Traumatic Stress Disorder or Military Sexual Trauma or both.

Many homeless persons are trapped in addictions. Others are developmentally disabled. A good number of the homeless are mentally ill.

Many have a combination of addiction, developmental disability and mental illness.

Released prisoners make up another huge fraction of the homeless; they are also subject to addiction, developmental disability and mental illness.

I continued to bring chocolate for the police officers. Kat and I continued to pray together at the beginning of each clinic.

Naturally, if you ask God to show you the face of Jesus in the face of each homeless person you serve, He answers your prayer. Soon I began to see Jesus in each of them.

A surprising thing began to happen: with no words spoken, the homeless men and women began to sense that I was seeing Jesus in them and they began to see Jesus in me. It was an incredibly sacred experience. More sacred than any other I have had before or since.

After two weeks it was time to begin my evening clinics at Austin Street Centre (ASC), a homeless shelter for men over 40 and for women and children of all ages. The shelter was funded by the Episcopal Church. After my afternoon shift at the Day Resource Center, I'd leave and drive a mile through seedy neighborhoods to get to ASC.

Austin Street Centre was surrounded by a wrought iron fence. I'd call the front desk from my cell phone and someone would come out to open the gate to allow me to park in their secure lot.

As I entered the huge building Kat was waiting. She introduced me to the front desk people. They were homeless men who were on permanent staff at the center. They greeted me warmly.

I saw a partitioned area straight past the front desk. Kat told me that this was where the women and their children stayed. She said that this was one of the only shelters where women were truly safe from assault by men. I followed Kat along the near wall to the back corner of the building. We passed 400 cots; most were filled with dozing men. A big screen TV was playing across the room.

There was an old church pew against the wall of our clinic in the back corner. The doctor whom I had shadowed had warned me to wear washable clothes when I worked at Austin Street. She said that the intake for the ventilation system for the clinic was near the smoking area and that a certain number of residents smoked crack cocaine there. I'd asked her what it smelled like and she just smiled and said, "You'll see."

I had bought a dark brown washable knit suit at Ross and had worn it that day. My purse was safe and invisible in the trunk of my car. My car key was on a lanyard around my neck. I carried a tote with forms and a book about psychiatric medications, a roll of paper towels and a spray bottle of Windex.

I entered the clinic area. My "office" was to be the small front room and the caseworkers would sit in the back room. An archway connected the two rooms. The back room contained a huge metal cupboard of paper files on the Austin Street patients.

As I set up, I noted that the table that would be my desk was filthy. I got out my bottle of Windex. I sprayed the table and wiped it dry four times before brown dirt stopped appearing on my paper towels. *Ugh!*

I turned the table so that its short edge was against the wall and pulled up the room's rolling chair. It did not fit me at all. I resolved to bring in one of my waiting room chairs and leave it so I would have a better chair to sit on during the clinic. I took out my forms and set up. The other workers were ready too. Kat showed in the first patient and introduced me. I flipped through his thick paper chart.

All of the men at this shelter were over 40. With few exceptions all of them had been homeless for a long time and none were considered able to be rehabilitated. Many considered the shelter their permanent home.

The men were turned out of the shelter at 7 a.m. and could not return until 4 p.m. This gave them time to walk the mile to the Stewpot for breakfast.

The women were at a great peril for assault and rape and they were only turned out for a short time while the shelter was thoroughly cleaned. Then they could return.

If the women wanted they could stay inside the wrought iron fence or in the chapel while waiting to come back inside. Women and children were fed breakfast and lunch.

I perused the man's chart. Most of the return patients at the shelter had thick charts and my job was to continue their medication as previously written. A few had side effects or new symptoms and then I had to change the medications.

This population was more stable than the more transient population at the Day Resource Center and there was less heartbreak in listening to their stories.

I saw nine men that first night and one woman, all returns.

The newness and the commotion of having the caseworkers so close by prevented me from doing much "Jesus sighting." This would come after a few weeks.

At the end of clinic we all packed up and returned to our cars.

My work was making me more and more grateful for all that I had.

Although I found working with the homeless the most gratifying work I had ever done, it exhausted me. I'd have enough energy to drive home and then I'd collapse, not good for much else the rest of the night.

When I got home that first night after the clinic at Austin Street I sniffed my suit. *Ugh and double ugh.* There was an odd smoky smell to the suit, just like the other doctor had predicted. I put right into the washer. *Note to self: always wear the brown suit on Thursdays.*

I soon decided to bring chocolate to the patients as well as the police. I gave each patient two Hershey kisses when he/she sat down to see me. Some told me that they looked forward to those Hershey's kisses the whole month.

The "police chocolate" paid off. If a patient so much as raised his voice a uniformed officer appeared in my doorway within ten seconds.

My afternoon clinic at the Day Resource Center was booming. Soon Hope asked me to do Thursday mornings as well. That clinic filled quickly and we added a Tuesday afternoon clinic. Within a month we added Tuesday morning as well.

I'd leave the house at 6:30 a.m. and drive into Dallas with little traffic. I'd sit in the parking lot across from the Day Resource Center and eat my breakfast and read the paper.

At 7:45 a.m. I'd go inside, give the police their chocolate and let myself into Hope's office. I'd clear her desk enough to work and get my forms and supplies ready. Kat would duck into "my" office and we would take a few minutes to pray.

At eight the police would let clinic patients into the building and they would sign a roster in the waiting room.

The waiting room also served as a connection between the two hallways where the team had offices. Kat would pull the paper charts on the repeat patients. Caseworkers would interview new patients and get them into the system.

We would close down for a short time at lunch to allow the patients to go over to the Stewpot for lunch. I'd close Hope's door and eat my lunch, more grateful than ever before for the blessing of having regular meals.

After a few months I began to feel really comfortable with the homeless. I felt able to address their psychiatric needs, including special needs like an increased dose of sleeping medicine in mosquito season; the pesky insects kept the homeless sleeping outside awake.

I began to hear a few of them express remorse for bad things they had done. I xeroxed a large print version of Psalm 51, King David's psalm of repentance after the Bathsheba incident. If a homeless person expressed remorse for any act, I would pull out a copy of the psalm and invite him to read it to me as I finished my note. If they felt better (they all felt better) I invited them to read it and reread it until they felt "clean." If they were a non-reader I would help them make a plan to have a friend read the psalm to them.

Almost all of the homeless experienced great relief from using Psalm 51. I decided to call it "Baptist Confession," as most of the homeless in Dallas are Baptist and would not imagine using "sacramental confession."

One person in particular had a startling change in appearance after using the psalm at home until she felt "clean."

She was a tall, red-headed woman with coal black eyes. I had worked with her for many months and had noted that no light seemed to shine from her eyes. I asked her if she had done something terrible. "Yes, ma'am," she said. I asked if she wanted to tell me what she had done, but she did not (most did want to tell me). After she read Psalm 51 she felt better. She took it to her housing and read it ten times before she felt clean. When she returned the next month she had greenish brown eyes that sparkled with light!

Soon, in the context of medication checks and psychiatric evaluations, I was able to attend to the spiritual needs of my patients as well as their medical and psychiatric needs.

I did this work on Tuesdays and Thursdays for six years. At the end of that time I was flat-out exhausted. I had caught walking pneumonia for the previous two winter seasons; this robbed me of all of my evening hours for eight weeks each time. With a heavy heart I resigned.

I still go to Austin Street Centre to serve dinner with my church. My "homies" still come up to me and thank me for the care I provided. I tell them it was an honor to serve them.

Mother Teresa was right; I didn't have to go to Calcutta. I found the poorest of the poor right in my town. I found the face of Jesus in each of them. I loved each one of them with the love of the Lord.

Right now my ministry is the writing of this book to share my experience, strength and hope at regaining my faith after clergy sex abuse. When I am done with this, I will perform "tasks as assigned," always trying to avoid the two by four.

finding a penny
outside the homeless shelter
leaving it

THIRTY FOUR

2010, Return to Planet Pecos

In July 2010, I decided to go back to Pecos for a few days.

I had visited Pecos with Sarah, Robin and Linda (Robin's mom), for several days in 1997. The turkey was gone by then; a variety of meats was served. I was able to fulfill my promise to take Sarah to Harry's. She still has the Harry's tee shirt I bought her that day.

In 1999 I visited Pecos for one night after giving a retreat in Albuquerque.

Now in 2010 I had made a reservation for four nights over the Fourth of July weekend. I made the 11-hour drive, leaving at 5 a.m.

When I got to New Mexico I noticed that the red hills were green; the vegetation near the road was very lush. I realized there had been an unusual amount of rain that year.

I made it to Pecos during the dinner hour and hurried up the stairs. There was a chair free next to Sister Miriam. I greeted her and we began to chat. I got the hairy eyeball from several others at the table. Later I learned that conversation was allowed only at lunch.

Miriam said that the reformer Abbots had taken the School away from the Community and had brought in teachers from other monasteries.

She smiled and said that Pecos was again a double monastery; nuns were welcome there again. I had read on the internet that most of the nuns, who had been stripped of their standing as nuns, had left for communities that would accept their vows. Miriam had refused to leave. I had seen online that one of the reformer Abbots had tried to persuade her to accept a bit of property on the grounds to honor her service. She refused and stayed planted in the nuns' dorm. *Go, girl!*

The Community was sparse. Seven monastics: Miriam; an elderly priest who had tended the bees when I was there in '95; a brother from before who was serving as Superior. The monastics I didn't recognize included one nun and three monks.

After dinner, soup and fresh biscuits, I returned to my room, #19, to unpack. As I walked down the hall I noted the warm golden tan of the hallway. Without thinking about it, I had painted my hallway at home the same color! Unpacking, I looked at the butter colored walls. My office and the room where I cocoon at night were both painted the same color. Score two for the unconscious mind.

When the bell for Compline sounded I trotted down the hall. The chapel had changed quite a bit. All of the glass was now clear; there was a new mural of Mary where the Guadalupe mural had been; the mosaic of the Risen Christ was now on the wall with His back to the river; the altar was now near the wall facing the nuns' dormitory.

The metal chairs had been replaced by beautiful custom-made wooden chairs with stepped upper edges that echoed the stepped adobe pillars outside. And there was only one box of Kleenex in the whole chapel.

My friend BA had visited the monastery with her husband in 2000 and had written that there was no music at Pecos any longer.

BA's remark about the music and the single box of Kleenex should have tipped me off that little emotion would be present in the services.

Still I was shocked at the lack of feeling in the liturgy. One of the monks was designated to read the psalm verse each day. He said the words, "I will praise you with timbrel and harps" as if it were part of the Burial Office.

I imagine that the liturgies at Pecos are now perfectly standard Benedictine liturgies. However, it was an intense disappointment to me having come to expect joyful worship there.

I walked down to the Pecos River after dinner and stood on the bridge. The water was clear, the stones on the bottom clearly visible.

I walked past the duck pond without stopping; there were no more graham crackers in the break room. I returned to the guesthouse. I unpacked and turned in early.

I made no attempt to walk in the morning.

The reformers had reintroduced most of the standard Benedictine offices. In the morning at 6:30 was the office of Vigils; 7:00 was Lection Divina/Meditation and 7:30 was Eucharist. Lauds or Praise had been eliminated. The noon prayer service had been reintroduced. I also noted that the monks now wore robes at all times. When I was at the School they only wore them for Eucharist.

I must say that the other retreatants, who all appeared to be nuns and priests, seemed very happy with the emotion-free worship.

I missed the joyful worship at the '95-96 Pecos. I missed the kind of worship that stirred things up. That necessitated lots of Kleenex. That healed you.

We went upstairs to our silent breakfast. Hard cooked eggs and fresh biscuits. I finished and dashed to my car.

I was meeting a haiku friend at Harry's for brunch. An old friend; he had recently moved back home to New Mexico. Harry's had changed! The parking lot now wraps around three sides of the building. The front is landscaped with a lush flower garden. Harry's is now a sprawling complex of rooms, including a bar. There are still a few tables outside where you can commune with hummingbirds and butterflies. The food is still fabulous. I had a wonderful salad and watermelon lemonade.

I visited the tiny church on the way back to the monastery. The hillside was covered in grass, another sign that it had been a wet year. In past years it had been purple-red dirt with no vegetation.

I drove into Renate's parking lot on the way back. Renate's sign was still up, and her lace curtains were still in the windows but the restaurant was gone. A realtor's sign was planted near the road.

I returned to the monastery in time for Mid-day Prayer and lunch. In the dining room I conversed a bit with two monks that I didn't know. I spoke briefly to Miriam on the way out.

I went for a walk. I walked along the long corridor of the monastery and exited toward the nuns' residence. A European-looking lady was working on the flower beds, which were lush with every color of bloom. I stepped up onto the dirt road and walked back to the guesthouse.

I holed up in my room, coming out only for the soup and biscuit dinner. I turned in early and set my alarm for an early departure. One day turned out to be enough for me.

I got up at five, showered and threw my things into the trunk. It had rained in the night. The upstream part of the laughing creek had overflowed, covering Highway 63 with red mud. I drove slowly through town. The Pecos had also overflowed with the rain; I crossed another skin of red mud. On the way to the Interstate I crossed the Pecos again. I would cross it three more times before I got home.

The sky was black most of the day. When approaching my turnoff for home the sun came out again and I saw a white dove flying from left to right across the road; the sun made her feathers radiant. To my far left was a double rainbow. I relaxed. *A descending dove and a rainbow! A double rainbow!*

I am grateful Planet Pecos was there for me when I needed it. I received enormous healing there. Persistent healing. Healing I have passed on to others. But the monastery that healed me is gone.

When I was at Pecos in rainy 2010 I stood under the cottonwood tree by the gift shop, listening to the leaves. I looked down. Moss!! I bent over to have a better look. Eleven small circles of moss, each no bigger that my pinky fingernail. How many decades did the spores remain dormant waiting for this rainy year?

The seeds of the Spirit are still at Pecos and maybe, someday, the Holy Spirit will be invited back to that monastery.

Meanwhile, both heavy sets of double wooden doors into the monastery are still carved with descending doves.

I hope the Spirit comes back. And I hope the Spirit brings along a truckload of Kleenex.

    her breast
    shining with the sun
    the descending dove

ACKNOWLEDGMENTS

Words cannot begin to express my gratitude to Mother Delores (not her real name), the Episcopal priest who served as my Confessor and Spiritual Director for 20 years. I would not be the woman I am today without her guidance and compassion. She knows who she is.

I thank my daughter, Sarah, for being the best thing that ever happened to me. I look forward to more of our special version of love, companionship and geek jokes.

I thank my late friend, JoAnn Stephens, prayer partner extraordinaire, friend, companion and pinch-hitter with my Sarah when I could not be there. I can't wait to see you again, JoAnn!

I thank all of my friends, clergy and lay, who encouraged me to go to Pecos. The Pecos of the mid-nineties was all they said and more.

I thank my friend Linda from the bottom of my heart for keeping Sarah while I was at Pecos. And I thank Robin for being such a good friend to Sarah, then and now.

I thank my friends who studied the healing ministry with me, especially JoAnn, her husband Dick, Nancy and her husband Dick, Sandy, Jimmy, Cheryl, and Jennifer. I also thank my late friends Bob and Julie; I can't wait to see you again Bob and Julie!

I thank my friends Matthew, Dennis and Sheila Linn, whose retreats and friendship were crucial in helping me with my rocky transition back to Jesus. Jesuits are good at that.

I thank the monastic community of Pecos as it was in the mid '90s. And I thank my classmates in the School for Charismatic Spiritual Directors, especially Coy, Michael, Bette Ann, Ann and Teal. I am exceedingly grateful to the Community and to these friends for providing a corrective emotional experience that has largely wiped away the tragic experience of my early childhood. I especially thank the priest Spiritual Directors at Pecos, and Coy and Michael for being unfailingly respectful gentlemen.

I thank my readers Beverly, Jane, Lorna, Andrea, Nell, Marsha, Lisa and Katherine for their amazing, helpful comments about the manuscript. I especially thank Marsha, Lisa and Katherine for reading chapters along the way.

I thank Frank, Carlos and Brian for copyediting the book. I thank Brian for designing the book in its printed form and making it so gorgeous. I thank Yolanda for her beautiful cover design.

I thank God for the Near Death Experience that occurred at the very end of the year I was abused. I am sure that my trip to heaven contributed significantly to my healing.

I thank God for asking me to write this book and for giving me the grace to do it. I ask Him to send this book into the hands of each of those He wants to read it.

I am confident that my abuser, Father Michael, is very much in favor of this book. I believe that in his death, when he was enfolded in the love of Jesus, he was healed completely. I believe that he deeply regrets what he did to me. I look forward to seeing you again, Michael!

RESOURCES FOR SURVIVORS AND SUPPORTERS

SNAP, the Survivor's Network of those Abused by Priests is the largest, oldest and most active support group for women and men wounded by religious authority figures (priests, ministers, bishops, deacons, nuns and others). Visit www.snapnetwork.org to locate a support group near you. SNAP has a national meeting each summer, a real resource if you live far from a SNAP support group.

BishopAccountability.org offers a searchable database of materials uncovered in civil suits against the Roman Catholic Church. It also has a searchable database of credibly accused priests. www.bishopaccountability.org

NSAC, the National Survivor's Advocate Coalition is a confederation of men and women of goodwill and conscience who are linked in the common pursuit of justice for survivors of clergy sex abuse by clergy of any denomination. NSAC offers an email newsletter M-F with updates on breaking clergy sex abuse stories around the globe. http://nationalsurvivoradvocatescoalition.wordpress.com/

Voice from the Desert works for healing and justice for survivors of sexual abuse, especially those who suffered childhood sexual abuse by priests and other religious authority figures in the Roman Catholic Church. Voice from the Desert examines the cover up, causes and effects of clergy sex abuse. Most importantly, Voice from the Desert promotes the safety of children. www.reform-network.net

Road to Recovery is the only non-profit in the US that offers compassionate counseling and referral services to survivors of clergy sex abuse. Road to Recovery assists survivors with emotional, psychological, financial and spiritual needs as they recover from clergy sex abuse. www.road-to-recovery.org

Note: All of the royalties from sales of this book will go to these non-profits.

BOOK: Jaime J. Romo, Ed.D, *Healing the Sexually Abused Heart: A Workbook for Survivors, Thrivers and Supporters.* This book is especially helpful for those who live far from a SNAP support group. www.jaimeromo.com

CD: John Michael Talbot's *The Lover and the Beloved* is based on the poems of St. John of the Cross, a mystic from the 1400s. These poems, found in St. John's book, *Dark Night of the Soul*, are set to music by Talbot. This music is astonishingly comforting in times of spiritual darkness, including the dark night of the soul.

Book: St. John of the Cross' book, *Dark Night of the Soul*, is available free online.

ABOUT THE AUTHOR

Susan Delphine Delaney MD, MS is a psychiatrist practicing in Plano, Texas. She is assisted in that work by her therapy dog Gabriella, a Bichon Frise.

Her first book, *Rx for Quilters*, sold 25,000 copies and was a Main Selection of the Doubleday Cooking and Crafts book of the Month Club.

Susan has published many magazine articles and two magazine columns. She is a haiku poet of international renown.

Made in the USA
Middletown, DE
25 October 2015